America's Best-Loved

Community Cookbook Recipes

Brunches & Lunches

Better Homes and Gardens®

Better Homes and Gardens® Books
Des Moines

Better Homes and Gardens® Books
An Imprint of Meredith® Books

America's Best Loved Community Cookbook Recipes
Brunches & Lunches
Editor: Christopher Cavanaugh
Associate Art Director: Lynda Haupert
Designer: Jeff Harrison
Copywriter: Kim Gayton Elliott
Copyeditor: Kathy Roberts
Production Manager: Doug Johnston

Editor-in-Chief: James D. Blume
Director, New Product Development: Ray Wolf
Test Kitchen Director: Sharon Stilwell

Better Homes and Gardens® Magazine
Editor-in-Chief: Jean LemMon
Executive Food Editor: Nancy Byal

Meredith Publishing Group
President, Publishing Group: Christopher M. Little
Vice President and Publishing Director: John P. Loughlin

Meredith Corporation
Chairman and Chief Executive Officer: Jack D. Rehm
President and Chief Operating Officer: William T. Kerr

Chairman of the Executive Committee: E.T. Meredith III

On the cover: Blueberry Buckle, see page 14; Morning Glory Muffins, see page 38; Fresh Fruit Trifle, see page 141

Our seal assures you that every recipe in **America's Best-Loved Community Cookbook Recipes** *Brunches & Lunches* has been tested in the *Better Homes and Gardens® Test Kitchen.* This means that each recipe is practical and reliable, and meets our high standards of taste appeal. We guarantee your satisfaction with this book for as long as you own it.

brunches & lunches

Anything goes!—that's the motto for brunch and lunch. Whether you choose to serve sweet breads, muffins, and egg-based dishes or rib-sticking sandwiches and hearty sides, the rules for these creative meals are completely flexible. Discover a little bit of everything yummy in this volume of Better Homes and Gardens® *America's Best-Loved Community Cookbook Recipes*.

For a traditional yet sensational Sunday brunch, partner Apple Streusel Muffins with Ham Alexandria and Fresh Pineapple and Strawberries in Shells. To create a down-home, soul-warming spread, try Old-Fashioned Potato Bread with Chicken Brunch Casserole and Three-Lettuce Salad. Warm weather requires a lighter touch, so Lemon Tea Bread, Crispy Corn Sticks, Cold Ham and Cheese Crepes, and a Fresh Fruit Trifle are called front and center. Mixing and matching the remarkable dishes in *Brunches & Lunches* is just part of the fun—the satisfaction of your family and friends will provide happy memories for years to come.

These extraordinary recipes come from all over the country, from families and communities just like yours—Bubble Bread was discovered by Leola Stone at a family reunion; melt-in-your-mouth Sour Milk Biscuits were first contributed by Bertha LaBombard to a community supper in 1819; June Gold was given her recipe for Noodle Kugel by her new mother-in-law; and Fruit Pizza is the inspired result of cooking by committee of the Junior League of Salt Lake City. The dishes are spectacular; the stories behind the dishes make them even more special.

contents

coffee cakes
& sweet breads

How sweet it is . . . waking up to a fragrant goody, fresh from the oven. Tender breads, muffins, coffee cakes, buns, and buckles are all represented in this mouthwatering array of brunchtime delicacies. Tempt your family with irresistibly wholesome Morning Glory Muffins, bursting with carrots, apples, and nuts, or lure them to the table with Cinnamon-Raisin Oatmeal Bread. Having friends to brunch? Try these eye-openers: Stuffed French Toast, Southern-style Bourbon Pecan Bread, or traditional Hot Cross Buns. From fun-to-pull-apart Bubble Bread to luscious Peach Coffee Cake, we'll help you greet the day in culinary style.

SOUR CREAM COFFEE CAKE

SOUR CREAM COFFEE CAKE

Makes 12 to 16 Servings

Cake:
1	cup margarine *or* butter
2	cups granulated sugar
2	eggs
1	8-ounce carton dairy sour cream
½	teaspoon vanilla
2	cups all-purpose flour
1	teaspoon baking powder
¼	teaspoon salt
¼	teaspoon baking soda

Topping:
½	cup chopped nuts
3	tablespoons brown sugar
2	tablespoons granulated sugar
2	teaspoons ground cinnamon

◆   ◆   ◆

LaRue Powell said that she makes her Sour Cream Coffee Cake all the time. "I like this cake so much that it is the only cake I make!" The recipe originally came from a co-worker several years ago, and LaRue said it has become a family favorite. If you don't want such a sweet cake, LaRue suggests that you omit the topping.

LaRue Powell
Laboratory Approved Recipes
Pathology Laboratories Wake
Medical Center
Raleigh
NORTH CAROLINA

1 Preheat the oven to 350°. Grease a 13x9x2-inch baking pan; set aside.

2 To make the cake: In a large mixing bowl, cream together the margarine or butter and the 2 cups granulated sugar with an electric mixer on medium speed. Add the eggs, sour cream and vanilla; beat for 1 minute more.

3 In a small bowl, stir together the flour, baking powder, salt and baking soda. Add the flour mixture to the sour cream mixture. Beat with the mixer on low speed for 2 to 3 minutes or until all the ingredients are combined.

4 To make the topping: In another small bowl, stir together the nuts, brown sugar, the 2 tablespoons granulated sugar and the cinnamon.

5 Pour *half* of the batter into the prepared baking pan. Sprinkle *half* of the topping over the batter in the pan. Spoon the remaining batter into the pan, spreading it slightly over the first layer of topping. Sprinkle the remaining topping over all.

6 Bake the coffee cake in the 350° oven about 35 minutes or until a wooden toothpick inserted near the center comes out clean. Cool slightly before serving.

 TIPS FROM OUR KITCHEN

Make this breakfast cake easier by preparing as much as you can the night before. In this recipe, you can measure the margarine or butter and granulated sugar into 1 mixing bowl, combine the dry ingredients in another bowl and stir together the topping ingredients in a third bowl. Cover all of the containers and leave them on the counter overnight. The next morning, preheat the oven and complete the preparations.

To warm any leftover cake: Place 1 piece on a microwave-safe plate and micro-cook, uncovered, on 100% power (high) for 15 to 20 seconds.

If desired, serve this coffee cake with sliced fruit.

Try the topping from this recipe sprinkled over ice cream or other frozen desserts.

Nutrition Analysis (*Per Serving*): Calories: 436 / Cholesterol: 44 mg / Carbohydrates: 54 g / Protein: 5 g / Sodium: 281 mg / Fat: 24 g (Saturated Fat: 6 g) / Potassium: 105 mg.

JEWISH APPLE CAKE

Makes 12 Servings

⅓   cup granulated sugar
2   teaspoons ground cinnamon
5 to 6 apples, peeled and thinly sliced (6 cups)
3   cups all-purpose flour
2½   cups granulated sugar
3   teaspoons baking powder
½   teaspoon salt
1   cup cooking oil
⅓   cup orange juice
2   teaspoons vanilla
4   eggs
Powdered Sugar Icing:
1   cup sifted powdered sugar
¼   teaspoon vanilla
1   teaspoon milk *or* orange juice
Milk *or* orange juice

◆   ◆   ◆

The Family Life Center is an organization dedicated to aiding women during pregnancy by providing prenatal care, maternity and baby clothing, career exploration, parenting classes, childbirth education classes and nutrition classes among many other services.

Karen Doswell
First Fruits
Family Life Center
Fort Walton Beach
FLORIDA

1 Preheat the oven to 350°. Grease and flour a 10-inch tube pan; set aside.

2 In a large bowl, stir together the ⅓ cup granulated sugar and the cinnamon. Add the apple slices; toss to coat with the sugar and cinnamon; set aside.

3 In another large bowl, stir together the flour, the 2½ cups granulated sugar, the baking powder and salt until well blended. Add the cooking oil, orange juice, the 2 teaspoons vanilla and the eggs; stir until smooth.

4 Pour *some* of the batter into the prepared pan; layer *some* of the coated apple slices over the batter in the pan. Repeat, alternating the batter with the coated apple slices, ending with a layer of the coated apple slices.

5 Bake in the 350° oven about 1½ hours or until a wooden toothpick inserted near the center of the cake comes out clean. (The cake may take as long as 2 hours to bake, depending upon the oven and the pan used.) Remove the cake from the oven; set on a wire rack and cool for 15 minutes. Carefully loosen the edges of the cake from the pan; invert the cake onto a serving plate and remove the pan. Let the cake stand for 2 hours.

6 Just before serving, make the Powdered Sugar Icing: In a small bowl, stir together the powdered sugar and the ¼ teaspoon vanilla. Stir in the 1 teaspoon milk or orange juice, adding additional milk or orange juice as necessary to make a drizzling consistency. Drizzle the icing over the cake.

 TIPS FROM OUR KITCHEN

Any type of baking or all-purpose apple can be used in this recipe. Try Cortland, Crispin, Criterion, Fuji, Golden Delicious, Granny Smith, Jonagold, Jonathan, Northern Spy, Rome Beauty, Winesap or York Imperial. Since the apples are peeled and sliced, you can use reduced-price bruised or "seconds" apples, if desired.

To quickly slice the apples, try a food processor. Cut the peeled apple halves to fit into the feed tube of the processor.

Nutrition Analysis (*Per Serving*): Calories: 536 / Cholesterol: 71 mg / Carbohydrates: 86 g / Protein: 5 g / Sodium: 115 mg / Fat: 21 g (Saturated Fat: 3 g) / Potassium: 129 mg.

BLUEBERRY BUCKLE

PEACH COFFEE CAKE

PEACH COFFEE CAKE

Makes 8 Servings
Cake:
   ½   cup butter *or* margarine
   ⅓   cup sugar
   1   teaspoon vanilla
   1   egg, beaten
 1½   cups all-purpose flour
 1½   teaspoons baking powder
   ¼   teaspoon salt
   ½   cup milk
Topping:
   1   8-ounce can sliced peaches, drained
   ¼   cup packed brown sugar
   2   tablespoons melted butter *or* margarine

♦ ♦ ♦

When volunteers at The General Hospital Center found it necessary to raise funds for their new uniforms, Alice Bock and her co-volunteers wrote their favorite recipes on the backs of greeting cards and sold them in the hospital lobby. The recipes were later published in <u>Always by Your Side</u>. This Peach Coffee Cake had already been taste-tested—and enjoyed—by the group!

Alice Bock
<u>Always by Your Side</u>
The General Hospital Center
Passaic
NEW JERSEY

1 Preheat oven to 350°. Grease an 8x8x2-inch baking pan.

2 To make the cake: In a large bowl, cream the ½ cup butter or margarine, sugar and vanilla together with an electric mixer. Add the egg and beat well.

3 In a small bowl, stir together the dry ingredients. Add the dry ingredients to the butter-sugar mixture alternately with the milk.

4 Spread the batter into the prepared pan. Top with the sliced peaches. Sprinkle with the brown sugar and drizzle with the melted butter.

5 Bake in the 350° oven for 30 to 35 minutes or until done.

TIPS FROM OUR KITCHEN

If the batter starts to climb your beaters as you're putting together this recipe, add the rest of the flour mixture by hand.

Don't worry about leftovers. They're easy to heat in the microwave oven. Just micro-cook, one piece at a time, on 100% power (high) for 15 seconds.

Nutrition Analysis (*Per Serving*): Calories: 297 / Cholesterol: 66 mg / Carbohydrates: 37 g / Protein: 4 g / Sodium: 287 mg / Fat: 16 g (Saturated Fat: 9 g) / Potassium: 105 mg.

LEMON TEA BREAD

Makes 1 Loaf (16 Servings)
Bread:
- ½ cup butter *or* margarine, softened
- 1 cup granulated sugar
- 2 eggs
- 1 teaspoon finely shredded lemon peel
- 1½ cups all-purpose flour
- 1 teaspoon baking powder
- ½ cup milk
- ½ cup chopped pecans

Lemon Glaze:
- ¼ cup granulated sugar
- 3 tablespoons lemon juice
- 1 teaspoon finely shredded lemon peel

Orange Cream Cheese:
- 1 8-ounce package cream cheese, softened
- ¼ cup sifted powdered sugar
- 1 tablespoon orange juice
- 1 teaspoon finely shredded orange peel

❖ ❖ ❖

Dorothy Huckabee found Lemon Tea Bread about six or seven years ago and then "just put it together with the cream cheese-and-juice spread." Dorothy often made Lemon Tea Bread for Junior League meetings and coffee gatherings.

Dorothy Huckabee
Under the Mulberry Tree
Esther Circle of the United
Methodist Women
Macon
GEORGIA

1 To make the bread: Preheat the oven to 350°. Grease and flour the bottom and halfway up the sides of an 8x4x2-inch loaf pan; set aside.

2 In a large mixing bowl, cream the softened butter or margarine and the 1 cup granulated sugar together with an electric mixer until fluffy. Add the eggs and the 1 teaspoon lemon peel. Beat the mixture well. Stir together the flour and baking powder. Add the flour-baking powder mixture to the sugar mixture alternately with the milk, beating well after each addition. Stir in the chopped pecans.

3 Spread the batter in the prepared loaf pan and bake in the 350° oven for 55 to 60 minutes or until a wooden toothpick inserted near the center of the bread comes out clean. If necessary, cover the bread with aluminum foil for the last 15 minutes of baking to prevent overbrowning.

4 Meanwhile, to make the Lemon Glaze: Stir together the ¼ cup granulated sugar, the lemon juice and the 1 teaspoon lemon peel. Spoon the Lemon Glaze over the hot bread. Cool in the pan for 10 minutes. Remove the bread from the pan and cool on a wire rack.

5 To make the Orange Cream Cheese: In a small bowl, stir together the cream cheese, powdered sugar, orange juice and orange peel until the mixture is well blended. Serve the Orange Cream Cheese with the Lemon Tea Bread.

 TIPS FROM OUR KITCHEN

To avoid rims around the top edge of the baked bread, grease the bottom and only halfway up the sides of the loaf pan.

You'll need 1 lemon for the juice and shredded peel called for in this recipe. For the best results, leave the lemon at room temperature for 30 minutes, then roll it on the counter under the palm of your hand to encourage the juice flow.

Nutrition Analysis (*Per Serving*): Calories: 239 / Cholesterol: 58 mg / Carbohydrates: 27 g / Protein: 4 g / Sodium: 114 mg / Fat: 14 g (Saturated Fat: 7 g) / Potassium: 70 mg.

LEMON TEA BREAD

Cinnamon-Raisin Oatmeal Bread

CINNAMON-RAISIN OATMEAL BREAD

Makes 2 Loaves (32 Servings)

- 1½ cups milk
- 1 cup uncooked rolled oats
- 1 cup raisins
- ¼ cup sugar
- ¼ cup shortening *or* cooking oil
- 1 teaspoon salt
- 2 packages active dry yeast
- ½ cup lukewarm water (105° to 115°)
- 1 egg, beaten
- 5¼ to 5¾ cups sifted all-purpose flour
- 1 tablespoon milk
- ½ cup sugar
- 2 tablespoons ground cinnamon
- 1 tablespoon melted butter *or* margarine

◆   ◆   ◆

Marian Jernigan thinks that she received this recipe, which she's had for many years, from her mother. This was one of Marian's favorite bread recipes because of the raisins and the oatmeal. She often made Cinnamon-Raisin Oatmeal Bread for her children and they loved it—it's very nutritious and has a wonderful taste.

Marian Jernigan
Our Favorite Recipes
Hope Lutheran Church
Moose Lake
MINNESOTA

1 In a small saucepan, scald the 1½ cups milk (just until small bubbles start to form around the edge of the pan).

2 In a large bowl, stir together the oats, raisins, the ¼ cup sugar, the shortening or cooking oil and salt. Pour the scalded milk over the oat mixture and stir until combined. Let the mixture cool.

3 Dissolve the yeast in the lukewarm water and add it to the cooled oat mixture. Add the beaten egg. Using a wooden spoon, stir in as much of the flour as you can.

4 On a lightly floured surface, knead the dough for 6 to 8 minutes or until smooth, adding enough of the remaining flour to make a moderately stiff dough.

5 Shape the dough into a ball and place it in a greased bowl, turning the dough once to grease the surface. Cover the bowl and let the dough rise in a warm place until doubled in size (about 45 minutes).

6 Punch the dough down; turn out onto a floured surface. Divide the dough in *half*. Cover and let rest for 10 minutes. Roll *each* half of the dough into a 15x10-inch rectangle. Brush *each* rectangle with the 1 tablespoon milk. In a small bowl, mix together the ½ cup sugar and the cinnamon. Sprinkle *half* of the cinnamon-sugar mixture over *each* dough rectangle.

7 Starting at a short side, tightly roll up the dough, jelly-roll fashion; seal the seams and tuck under the ends. Place each rolled loaf, seam side down, in a greased 9x5x3-inch loaf pan. Brush the tops of the loaves with the melted butter or margarine. Let the loaves rise until they are nearly doubled in size (about 45 minutes). Preheat the oven to 350°.

8 Bake in the 350° oven about 50 minutes or until the bread sounds hollow when lightly tapped.

 TIPS FROM OUR KITCHEN

The temperature of the water used with the yeast is important to the final results. Check the water with a thermometer; or, heat it in your microwave oven using the temperature probe.

Nutrition Analysis (*Per Serving*): Calories: 139 / Cholesterol: 8 mg / Carbohydrates: 25 g / Protein: 3 g / Sodium: 79 mg / Fat: 3 g (Saturated Fat: 1 g) / Potassium: 94 mg.

Bourbon Pecan Bread

Makes 2 Loaves (16 Servings)
- ¾   cup raisins
- ⅓   cup bourbon
- ⅔   cup butter *or* margarine, softened
- 1½   cups sugar
- 6   eggs, separated
- 2   cups all-purpose flour
- 1   cup coarsely broken pecans
- 1¼   teaspoons vanilla

◆   ◆   ◆

Cheeky Bahe views her collection of cookbooks with their handwritten notes as part of her family heritage. She remembers Bourbon Pecan Bread being served by her mother and grandmother at holidays when she was a child. Recently Breeder's Cup participants were greeted at the Louisville airport with samples of this delicious bread. What a nice welcome!

Cheeky Bahe
CordonBlueGrass
The Junior League of
Louisville, Inc.
Louisville
KENTUCKY

1 Soak the raisins in the bourbon for 30 minutes. Drain, reserving the bourbon. If necessary, add more bourbon to make ⅓ cup.

2 Preheat oven to 350°. Generously grease two 8x4x2-inch loaf pans and line the pan bottoms with greased waxed paper.

3 In a large bowl, cream the butter and *½ cup* of the sugar with an electric mixer until fluffy. Add egg yolks, one at a time, beating well.

4 Add the flour in thirds, alternating with the bourbon; mix until well blended.

5 Stir in the raisins, pecans and vanilla.

6 In a large bowl with clean beaters, beat the egg whites until soft peaks form (tips curl) when the beaters are raised. Gradually beat in the remaining sugar and beat until stiff peaks form (tips stand straight).

7 Fold about *2 cups* of the beaten egg whites into the batter to lighten it.

8 Gently fold the remaining beaten egg whites into the batter mixture.

9 Pour the batter into the prepared loaf pans. Bake in the 350° oven for 50 to 55 minutes or until a wooden toothpick inserted near the center comes out clean. Cool for 10 minutes. Remove the breads from the pans and cool on wire racks.

 Tips from Our Kitchen

Make this bread using almonds, walnuts or hazelnuts in place of the pecans. It will taste great no matter which nut you choose.

For an extra special presentation, drizzle this loaf with a thin powdered-sugar glaze and trim it with whole nuts.

Nutrition Analysis (*Per Serving*): Calories: 292 / Cholesterol: 100 mg / Carbohydrates: 36 g / Protein: 5 g / Sodium: 103 mg / Fat: 14 g (Saturated Fat: 6 g) / Potassium: 118 mg.

BOURBON PECAN BREAD

ORANGE DATE-NUT BREAD

ORANGE DATE-NUT BREAD

Makes 1 Loaf (18 Servings)

- 1 cup snipped dates
- 4 teaspoons finely shredded orange peel
- ⅔ cup boiling water
- ⅓ cup orange juice, freshly squeezed
- ¾ cup sugar
- 2 tablespoons shortening
- 1 beaten egg
- 1 teaspoon vanilla
- 2 cups all-purpose flour
- 1 teaspoon baking powder
- ½ teaspoon baking soda
- ¼ teaspoon salt
- ½ cup chopped nuts

✦ ✦ ✦

St. Melany's Byzantine Parish originally consisted of 35 families, and services were held in the homes of the parishioners. Eventually the growing parish found it necessary to move the services to a church. To help generate funds to purchase a building, the parishioners put together the Around the World Cookbook. *Chairperson Marcella Leight tells us that this project, "was a lot of hard work, but a lot of fun."*

Around the World Cookbook
St. Melany's Byzantine
Catholic Church
Tucson
ARIZONA

1 Preheat the oven to 350°. Grease a 9x5x3-inch loaf pan. Set aside.

2 In a large bowl, combine the snipped dates and shredded orange peel. Stir in the boiling water and orange juice.

3 Add the sugar, shortening, egg and vanilla, stirring until just mixed.

4 In a small bowl, stir together the flour, baking powder, baking soda and salt. Add the flour mixture to the date mixture and mix well. Stir in the nuts. Pour the batter into the prepared pan.

5 Bake in the 350° oven for 45 to 50 minutes or until a wooden toothpick inserted near the center comes out clean.

6 Cool the bread for 10 minutes in the pan. Then, remove the bread from the pan and cool thoroughly on a wire rack. Wrap and store the bread overnight.

 TIPS FROM OUR KITCHEN

Many quick-bread recipes suggest wrapping and storing the loaves overnight before slicing. This allows the flavors to mellow and also makes the loaves easier to slice. After baking, let the loaf cool completely on a wire rack, then wrap it in foil or plastic wrap and store at room temperature overnight.

Pre-chopped dates are available in many stores. They have a slight sugar coating to prevent them from sticking together in the package, but that won't affect the recipe. To snip the dates yourself, use kitchen shears. Dip the shears in water between snips.

Grease the loaf pan on the bottom and only 1 inch up the sides. This will eliminate a rim from forming around the edge of the baked loaf.

To make this recipe, you'll need one medium orange for the juice and peel. Choose an orange that feels heavy for its size and allow it to come to room temperature to get the most juice.

Nutrition Analysis: (*Per Serving*): Calories: 121 / Cholesterol: 12 mg / Carbohydrates: 21 g / Protein: 2 g / Sodium: 58 mg / Fat: 4 g (Saturated Fat: 1 g) / Potassium: 101 mg.

HONEY ORANGE BREAD

Makes 1 Loaf (12 Servings)

⅓	cup margarine *or* butter, softened
¾	cup honey
1	egg
1	tablespoon finely shredded orange peel
1¼	cups all-purpose flour
¾	cup whole wheat flour
½	cup unprocessed bran
1	tablespoon baking powder
½	teaspoon baking soda
½	teaspoon salt
¾	cup orange juice
¾	cup chopped walnuts

❖ ❖ ❖

A relative from Ohio gave Paulette Elmore this recipe for Honey Orange Bread many years ago. Paulette calls this an elegant bread that's excellent for a brunch or entertaining. Paulette likes cooking, but finds she seldom has enough time anymore. Therefore, the cooking has been passed along to her husband, who "seems to find convenient, less costly ingredients and has great organizational skills" in the kitchen.

Paulette Elmore
<u>Southern Elegance</u>
Junior League of Gaston County
Gastonia
NORTH CAROLINA

1 Preheat the oven to 325°. Grease only the bottom and halfway up the sides of a 9x5x3-inch loaf pan; set aside.

2 In a large mixing bowl using an electric mixer, cream together the softened margarine or butter and honey. Add the egg and shredded orange peel. Beat until the mixture is well blended.

3 In a medium bowl, stir together the all-purpose and whole wheat flours, bran, baking powder, baking soda and salt. Add the flour mixture and the orange juice alternately to the honey mixture, beating until the batter is smooth. Stir in the walnuts.

4 Pour the batter into the prepared pan. Bake in the 325° oven for 50 to 60 minutes or until a wooden toothpick inserted near the center of the bread comes out clean.

5 Set the pan on a wire rack; cool for 10 minutes. Remove the bread from the pan and cool on a wire rack. For easier slicing, wrap the bread in plastic wrap and let stand overnight.

 TIPS FROM OUR KITCHEN

Honey that has become crystallized or cloudy can be made clear and smooth again by setting the jar in a container of warm water. Stir the honey occasionally until the crystals dissolve; change the warm water as needed.

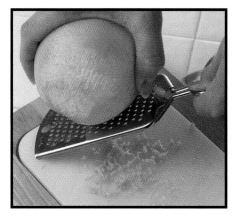

You'll need up to 3 medium oranges to yield the ¾ cup of fresh juice called for in this recipe. Before squeezing the oranges for juice, shred the peel from them using a fine shredder.

If the top of the loaf becomes too brown after being in the oven for 40 minutes, loosely cover it with aluminum foil for the rest of the baking time.

If desired, use a doily to create a patterned look on the top of the loaf of bread. To do so, place a doily on top and lightly sift powdered sugar over the doily. Then, carefully lift the doily from the loaf.

Nutrition Analysis (*Per Serving*): Calories: 249 / Cholesterol: 18 mg / Carbohydrates: 37 g / Protein: 4 g / Sodium: 299 mg / Fat: 11 g (Saturated Fat: 2 g) / Potassium: 163 mg.

HONEY ORANGE BREAD

STUFFED FRENCH TOAST

STUFFED FRENCH TOAST

Makes 10 Servings

10	1½-inch-thick slices French bread
1	8-ounce package cream cheese, softened
1	10-ounce jar apricot jam *or* orange marmalade
4	eggs
1	cup milk
2	tablespoons sugar
1	teaspoon vanilla
¼	teaspoon ground nutmeg *or* ground cinnamon
	Margarine, butter *or* cooking oil
	Maple-flavored syrup *or* maple syrup (optional)

♦   ♦   ♦

Very Innovative Parties is a source book for party inspiration. The cookbook includes sixty complete party ideas and 450 outstanding recipes, which range from quick and easy to gourmet. Profits from cookbook sales are used to help the Loma Linda University Dental Auxiliary in their efforts to support missionary work conducted by the health professions.

Very Innovative Parties
Loma Linda University Dental Auxiliary
Loma Linda
CALIFORNIA

1 Using a serrated knife, carefully cut a pocket in the middle of each bread slice, cutting ¾ of the way through.

2 Spread the cream cheese and jam or marmalade in each of the prepared pockets, dividing the full amount of both among the slices.

3 Place the stuffed slices, cut sides down, in a 13x9x2-inch baking pan.

4 In a small mixing bowl, beat together the eggs, milk, sugar, vanilla and nutmeg or cinnamon.

5 Pour *half* of the egg mixture over the slices and let stand until the bread has absorbed the mixture. Turn the slices over and pour the remaining egg mixture over the slices. Let stand until all of the egg mixture has been absorbed by the bread slices.

6 In a large skillet or on a griddle over medium heat, cook the stuffed bread in a small amount of hot margarine, butter or cooking oil for 2 to 3 minutes on each side or until golden brown. Add more margarine, butter or cooking oil as needed. Serve with syrup, if desired.

 TIPS FROM OUR KITCHEN

If you prefer to cook all the slices at once, try baking them. Place the soaked bread on a greased baking sheet. Bake in a 450° oven for 7 minutes. Turn the bread and bake 8 minutes more or until golden.

If desired, use reduced-fat cream cheese, skim milk and reduced-calorie syrup.

It may seem like the bread is stuffed with a lot of filling, but it won't be too much after the bread slices cook.

Pure maple syrup can be quite expensive because of the labor-intensive process involved in producing it. Maple-flavored syrup is less expensive because it is a combination of a less costly syrup, such as corn syrup, and a small amount of maple syrup. Pure maple syrup has a more subtle maple flavor, is thinner and is not as sweet as maple-flavored syrup.

Nutrition Analysis (*Per Serving*): Calories: 426 / Cholesterol: 112 mg / Carbohydrates: 60 g / Protein: 12 g / Sodium: 522 mg / Fat: 16 g (Saturated Fat: 7 g) / Potassium: 176 mg.

KOLACHES

Makes 24 Buns
Buns:
1	cup warm milk (110° to 115°)
1	package active dry yeast
1/3	cup cooking oil
1/4	cup sugar
1	egg
1/2	teaspoon salt
3 1/3 to 3 3/4	cups all-purpose flour

Cooking oil
Filling:
1	12-ounce package large prunes *or* 10 ounces pitted prunes
3/4	cup applesauce
2	tablespoons sugar
1/2	teaspoon vanilla
1/2	teaspoon ground cinnamon
1/4	teaspoon ground nutmeg

❖   ❖   ❖

The members of the Junior League of Kankakee County, Illinois, Inc. will soon be celebrating the organization's twenty-fifth year of community service—and they have good reason to celebrate. Their many worthwhile projects, have contributed approximately $363,000 to the community.

Mardene Hinton
Posh Pantry
The Junior League of Kankakee County, Illinois, Inc.
Kankakee
ILLINOIS

1 Grease 2 baking sheets; set aside.

2 To make the buns: In a large mixing bowl, stir together the warm milk and yeast until the yeast is dissolved. Add the 1/3 cup oil, the 1/4 cup sugar, the egg, salt and *2 cups* of the flour. Beat well. Add the remaining flour, a little at a time, to form a dough that is soft but not too sticky when touched. (Depending on conditions, you may use more or less flour.)

3 Shape the dough into a ball and place in a large, lightly greased bowl. Brush the top of the dough with *1 teaspoon* cooking oil and cover with a cloth. Let rise in a warm place until doubled in size (about 1 hour).

4 Meanwhile, to prepare the filling: In a medium saucepan, combine the prunes and enough *water* to cover. Bring to a boil. Reduce heat; cover and simmer about 20 minutes or until tender. Drain and cool. Remove the pits, if necessary. Using the back of a spoon, mash the prunes. Stir in the applesauce, the 2 tablespoons sugar, the vanilla, cinnamon and nutmeg. Set aside to cool.

5 Punch the dough down. Divide and shape the dough into twenty-four 1 1/2-

inch balls. Place on the prepared baking sheets, about 2 inches apart. Flatten each to a 2 1/2-inch circle. Brush the tops with oil; cover and let rise until almost doubled in size (about 30 minutes).

6 Preheat the oven to 425°. Using your thumb and 2 fingers, make an indentation in the center of each dough circle. Spoon about *1 tablespoon* of the filling into the center of *each* roll.

7 Bake in the 425° oven for 10 to 15 minutes or until golden brown. Remove from oven and transfer to wire racks to cool. When cool, store the rolls in airtight containers.

 TIPS FROM OUR KITCHEN

Sprinkle baked Kolaches with powdered sugar or drizzle with a powdered sugar glaze for a sweeter taste.

You may find that you'll have extra filling after completing the Kolaches. The filling is delicious spread over bread, toast, bagles or English muffins.

Nutrition Analysis (*Per Bun*): Calories: 163 / Cholesterol: 10 mg / Carbohydrates: 26 g / Protein: 3 g / Sodium: 33 mg / Fat: 6 g (Saturated Fat: 1 g) / Potassium: 153 mg.

KOLACHES

CINNAMON TWISTS

Cinnamon Twists

Makes 24 Servings

1	8-ounce carton dairy sour cream
3	tablespoons granulated sugar
1	package active dry yeast
½	teaspoon salt
⅛	teaspoon baking soda
1	large egg
2	tablespoons shortening, softened margarine *or* softened butter
2½ to 3	cups all-purpose flour
⅓	cup packed brown sugar
1	teaspoon ground cinnamon
2	tablespoons margarine *or* butter, melted

◆ ◆ ◆

Mary Ann Johnston told us that she and her brothers grew up eating their mom's Cinnamon Twists. Her mom had enjoyed the recipe for over forty years, but about twenty-five years ago, she lost the recipe. As soon as she found it again, Mary Ann made sure she got a copy. She says that "Once you've made Cinnamon Twists, preparing them becomes second nature."

Mary Ann Johnston
Easy Elegant Edibles
Rogers-Bentonville Junior
Auxiliary
Rogers
ARKANSAS

1 Preheat the oven to 375°. Lightly grease 2 baking sheets. Set aside.

2 In a small saucepan, heat and stir the sour cream just until warm. *(Do not boil.)* Remove from heat; transfer to a large mixing bowl and stir in the granulated sugar, yeast, salt and baking soda until they are dissolved.

3 Using a wooden spoon, stir in the egg; the 2 tablespoons shortening, softened margarine or butter; and as much of the flour as you can.

4 Turn the dough out onto a floured surface and knead in enough of the remaining flour to make a moderately stiff dough that is smooth and elastic (6 to 8 minutes total). Cover and let rest for 10 minutes.

5 In a small bowl, stir together the brown sugar and the cinnamon. Set aside.

6 On a lightly floured surface, roll out the dough to a 24x6-inch rectangle. Brush the dough with the 2 tablespoons melted margarine or butter and sprinkle the brown sugar-cinnamon mixture over *half* of the dough (lengthwise—a 24x3-inch area). Fold the area

of plain dough over the brown sug cinnamon mixture. Cut into twenty-four 1-inch-wide strips.

7 One at a time, hold the strips at both ends and twist in opposite directions. Place the twists on the prepared baking sheets, 2 inches apart, pressing both ends down. Cover and let the twists rise until almost doubled in size (45 to 60 minutes).

8 Bake in the 375° oven for 12 to 15 minutes or until lightly browned. Serve warm.

 TIPS FROM OUR KITCHEN

To reheat 1 twist, micro-cook on 100% power (high) for 10 to 12 seconds.

For easier rolling, divide the dough in half. Roll each half to a 12x6-inch rectangle.

Don't try to heat the sour cream in a microwave oven. It needs constant stirring during heating to avoid curdling.

Nutrition Analysis (*Per Serving*): Calories: 103 / Cholesterol: 16 mg / Carbohydrates: 14 g / Protein: 2 g / Sodium: 2314 mg / Fat: 4 g (Saturated Fat: 2 g) / Potassium: 46 mg.

OATMEAL-RAISIN SCONES

Makes 12 Scones

1	cup all-purpose flour
3	tablespoons packed brown sugar
1½	teaspoons baking powder
½	teaspoon ground cinnamon
⅓	cup margarine *or* butter
1	cup quick-cooking rolled oats
½	cup raisins, chopped
2	egg whites
¼	cup milk

All-purpose flour

2   teaspoons milk

Jelly *or* jam (optional)

❖   ❖   ❖

Jan Zinn is an excellent baker who loves trying new recipes. When she found this one for Oatmeal-Raisin Scones, she made it several times, changing the ingredients until she found the scone she liked best. Jan said that it's a nice sweet to serve with tea or coffee at mid-morning get-togethers. She finds Oatmeal Raisin-Scones unique because "they're low in fat and they taste wonderful."

Jan Zinn
<u>**First Fruits**</u>
Family Life Center
Fort Walton Beach
FLORIDA

1 Preheat the oven to 400°

2 In a large bowl, stir together the 1 cup flour, the brown sugar, baking powder and cinnamon. Using a pastry blender or 2 knives, cut in the margarine or butter until the mixture is crumbly. Stir in the rolled oats and chopped raisins.

3 In a small bowl, stir together the egg whites and the ¼ cup milk. Add the egg white mixture to the flour mixture and stir just until the ingredients are combined.

4 Turn the dough out onto a lightly floured surface. Roll or pat the dough into a 7-inch circle. Using a floured knife, cut the dough circle into 12 wedges; dip the knife into additional flour as often as necessary to keep the dough from sticking to the knife.

5 Transfer the dough wedges to an ungreased baking sheet. Brush the tops of the wedges with the 2 teaspoons milk. Bake in the 400° oven for 10 to 12 minutes or until the scones are golden. Serve the scones warm with the jelly or jam, if desired.

 TIPS FROM OUR KITCHEN

Scones are a biscuitlike quick bread often flavored with a variety of dried fruits or even miniature chocolate pieces. Traditionally, they are served split in half and spread with butter or preserves.

If the dough seems sticky and is difficult to work with, lightly grease your fingers before patting the dough into a circle.

You can substitute other dried fruits, such as snipped apricots, dates or cherries, for the raisins in this recipe. Chopped nuts can be used also.

To reheat 1 scone: Place it on a plate in a microwave oven and cook on 100% power (high) for 15 seconds.

Nutrition Analysis (*Per Scone*): Calories: 146 / Cholesterol: 0 mg / Carbohydrates: 21 g / Protein: 3 g / Sodium: 76 mg / Fat: 6 g (Saturated Fat: 1 g) / Potassium: 113 mg.

OATMEAL-RAISIN SCONES

35

APPLE STREUSEL MUFFINS

APPLE STREUSEL MUFFINS

Makes 18 Muffins

Muffins:

2	cups all-purpose flour
1	cup sugar
1¼	teaspoons ground cinnamon
1	teaspoon baking powder
½	teaspoon baking soda
½	teaspoon salt
2	eggs
1	8-ounce carton dairy sour cream
¼	cup margarine *or* butter, melted
1	cup finely chopped unpeeled apples

Streusel Topping:

¼	cup sugar
3	tablespoons all-purpose flour
¼	teaspoon ground cinnamon
2	tablespoons margarine *or* butter

♦ ♦ ♦

"You know how college kids are— they always love mom's cooking!" Mary Livelsberger often treated her children to Apple Streusel Muffins when they were home on college breaks, and the muffins were frequently part of a typical Livelsberger breakfast.

Mary Livelsberger
The Flavor and Spice
of Holy Cross Life
Holy Cross Parish
Batavia
ILLINOIS

1 Preheat the oven to 400°. Generously grease 18 muffin cups or line them with paper bake cups; set aside.

2 To make the muffins: In a large bowl, stir together the flour, sugar, cinnamon, baking powder, baking soda and salt.

3 In a small mixing bowl, beat the eggs. Stir in the sour cream and the ¼ cup melted margarine or butter. Add the egg mixture to the flour mixture along with the chopped apples. Stir just until moistened.

4 Spoon the batter into the prepared muffin cups filling them ⅔ full.

5 To make the Streusel Topping: In a small bowl, stir together the sugar, flour and cinnamon. Using a pastry blender, cut in the 2 tablespoons margarine or butter until the mixture resembles coarse crumbs. Sprinkle a portion of the topping on each muffin.

6 Bake the muffins in the 400° oven for 20 to 25 minutes or until the tops are golden.

TIPS FROM OUR KITCHEN

To reduce some of the fat and calories in these muffins, use light sour cream instead of the regular sour cream.

To reheat room-temperature muffins, wrap one in a paper towel and microcook on 100% power (high) for 15 to 20 seconds. To reheat frozen muffins, wrap one in a paper towel and microcook on 100% power (high) for 30 to 45 seconds.

When making muffins, avoid overstirring after the liquid ingredients are added; some lumps should remain. If you stir until the batter is smooth, the resulting muffins will have pointed tops, tunnels and a tougher texture.

Nutrition Analysis (*Per Muffin*): Calories: 176 / Cholesterol: 29 mg / Carbohydrates: 26 g / Protein: 3 g / Sodium: 142 mg / Fat: 7 g (Saturated Fat: 3 g) / Potassium: 50 mg.

MORNING GLORY MUFFINS

Makes 18 Muffins

- 2 cups all-purpose flour
- 1 cup sugar
- 2 teaspoons baking powder
- 2 teaspoons ground cinnamon
- ½ teaspoon baking soda
- ¼ teaspoon salt
- 2 cups finely shredded carrot
- 1 cup finely chopped apple
- ½ cup raisins
- ½ cup chopped nuts
- ½ cup shredded coconut
- 3 eggs
- ¾ cup cooking oil
- 2 teaspoons vanilla

◆ ◆ ◆

Ruth Matthews's recipe for Morning Glory Muffins is an old family favorite, given to her by her mother. Ruth tells us that she especially likes to serve the muffins around the holidays and to special visitors. We love this recipe just as it is, but if you'd like a different twist, try substituting shredded zucchini for all or part of the shredded carrot.

Ruth Matthews
What's Cooking at Northmont
Women's Christian Service Organization, Northmont United Presbyterian Church Pittsburgh
PENNSYLVANIA

1 Preheat the oven to 350°. Lightly grease eighteen 2½-inch muffin cups or line them with paper bake cups.

2 In a large mixing bowl, stir together the flour, sugar, baking powder, cinnamon, baking soda and salt. Stir in the carrot, apple, raisins, nuts and coconut.

3 In a separate bowl, stir together the eggs, cooking oil and vanilla. Add the liquid ingredients all at once to the flour mixture and stir just until moistened.

4 Gently spoon the batter into the prepared muffin cups until each one is almost full.

5 Bake in the 350° oven about 30 minutes or until the top of a muffin springs back when lightly touched. Cool in the pan set on a wire rack for 5 minutes. Remove the muffins from the pan and cool on the rack. Serve warm or at room temperature.

 TIPS FROM OUR KITCHEN

The fastest way to get two cups of shredded carrot is to use a food processor fitted with a shredding blade. Follow the directions that came with your machine. The finer the shred, the more readily the carrot will become part of the batter.

This batter is naturally lumpy due to all of the extra ingredients. When adding the liquid ingredients to the flour mixture, do not overmix or your muffins will have peaked tops and a tough, heavy texture.

Nutrition Analysis *(Per Muffin)*: Calories: 231 / Cholesterol: 36 mg / Carbohydrates: 28 mg / Protein: 3 g / Sodium: 101 mg / Fat: 12 g (Saturated Fat: 2 g) / Potassium: 132 mg.

MORNING GLORY MUFFINS

SIX-DAY MUFFINS

SIX-DAY MUFFINS

Makes 30 Muffins

3	cups whole bran cereal
2	cups buttermilk
1½	cups sugar
2	eggs, beaten
½	cup shortening, melted
2½	cups all-purpose flour
2½	teaspoons baking soda
½	teaspoon salt
½	cup snipped dates (optional)
½	cup raisins (optional)
½	cup chopped apple (optional)

◆   ◆   ◆

Karen Schrock Peachey received this recipe at a brunch meeting she attended several years ago. Now she serves her Six-Day Muffins at brunches she hosts. Karen says that it is important to her that her children eat well, so she starts their days with a fresh-baked muffin and a glass of juice. Our thanks to her for this healthy inspiration.

Mrs. Karen S. Schrock Peachey
<u>Magnolia Cookery</u>
Magnolia Mennonite Church
Macon
MISSISSIPPI

1 In a small mixing bowl, pour 1 cup *boiling water* over *1 cup* of the whole bran cereal. Set aside.

2 In a medium mixing bowl, combine the remaining *2 cups* bran cereal with the buttermilk, sugar, eggs and melted shortening.

3 Into a large mixing bowl, sift together the flour with the soda and salt. Make a well in the center.

4 Add the 2 bran mixtures all at once to the flour mixture. Stir just until moistened (batter will be lumpy). Store the batter in a covered container in the refrigerator up to 6 days.

5 To bake: Preheat oven to 400°. Gently stir in the dates, raisins, and/or chopped apple, if desired. Grease the desired number of muffin cups or line with paper bake cups. Fill each cup almost full. Bake the muffins in the 400° oven about 20 minutes or until golden.

TIPS FROM OUR KITCHEN

This muffin batter will store in the refrigerator up to six days. Or, if you prefer, bake the batter all at once and store the baked muffins in the freezer.

"Ledges on the edges" are those unwanted rims around the edges of your muffins. To get nicely rounded muffins without ledges, grease the muffin cups on the bottoms and only *halfway* up the sides.

To avoid soggy sides and bottoms, remove the muffins from their baking pans immediately.

To reheat muffins: Place them on a microwave safe plate and heat, uncovered, on 100% power (high) until warm. Allow 15 to 20 seconds for 1 to 2 muffins and 30 to 60 seconds for 4 muffins.

Nutrition Analysis *(Per Muffin)*: Calories: 134 / Cholesterol: 15 mg / Carbohydrates: 24 g / Protein: 3 g / Sodium: 222 mg / Fat: 4 g (Saturated Fat: 1 g) / Potassium: 144 mg.

SPICED CRANBERRY MUFFINS WITH ORANGE-HONEY BUTTER

Makes 18 Muffins
Muffins:

2	cups all-purpose flour
1	cup sugar
1½	teaspoons baking powder
1½	teaspoons ground nutmeg
1	teaspoon ground cinnamon
½	teaspoon baking soda
½	teaspoon ground ginger
½	cup shortening
2	teaspoons grated orange peel
¾	cup orange juice
2	eggs, slightly beaten
1	tablespoon vanilla
1½	cups coarsely chopped cranberries
1⅓	cups chopped walnuts

Orange-Honey Butter:

½	cup butter *or* margarine, softened
2	tablespoons honey
1	tablespoon grated orange peel

✦ ✦ ✦

Carol Ziemann conducts baking, cooking and holiday entertaining classes at a grocery store chain in St. Louis. This is one of her special holiday recipes that she finds especially unique because of the ginger and cranberry combination.

Carol Ziemann
<u>Gateways</u>
Auxiliary Twigs…Friends of the
St. Louis Children's Hospital
St. Louis
MISSOURI

1 Preheat the oven to 350°. Grease 18 muffin cups or line them with paper bake cups; set aside.

2 To make the muffins: In a large bowl, stir together the flour, sugar, baking powder, nutmeg, cinnamon, baking soda and ginger.

3 Using a pastry blender, cut the shortening into the flour mixture until the mixture is the consistency of coarse meal.

4 In a small bowl, mix together the 2 teaspoons orange peel, the orange juice, slightly beaten eggs and vanilla. Stir the egg mixture into the flour mixture just until the ingredients are moistened. Gently fold in the cranberries and *1 cup* of the walnuts.

5 Spoon the batter into the prepared muffin cups. Sprinkle the tops of the muffins with the remaining walnuts.

6 Bake the muffins in the 350° oven for 25 to 30 minutes or until a wooden toothpick inserted near the centers comes out clean.

7 Meanwhile, to make the Orange-Honey Butter: In a small mixing bowl, beat the softened butter or margarine with an electric mixer on medium speed until fluffy. Gradually beat in the honey and the 1 tablespoon orange peel.

8 Serve the muffins warm with the Orange-Honey Butter.

 TIPS FROM OUR KITCHEN

To keep the bottoms of the muffins from becoming soggy, immediately remove the muffins from the pans after baking and set them on a wire rack to cool.

If desired press the Orange-Honey Butter into a mold or fancy dish. Or, using a pastry bag fitted with a star tip, pipe the Orange-Honey Butter into individual serving dishes or onto plates.

Baked muffins can be frozen up to 3 months. To do so, wrap the muffins tightly in heavy-duty aluminum foil or place them in a freezer-safe plastic bag. To reheat frozen muffins, wrap them in heavy-duty aluminum foil and bake in a 300° oven for 15 to 18 minutes.

Nutrition Analysis (*Per Muffin*): Calories: 275 / Cholesterol: 37 mg / Carbohydrates: 28 g / Protein: 3 g / Sodium: 84 mg / Fat: 18 g (Saturated Fat: 5 g) / Potassium: 110 mg.

SPICED CRANBERRY MUFFINS WITH ORANGE-HONEY BUTTER

HOT CROSS BUNS

HOT CROSS BUNS

Makes 20 Buns
Buns:

1	cup milk
⅓	cup sugar
⅓	cup shortening
½	teaspoon salt
2	packages active dry yeast
¼	cup lukewarm water
2	eggs, beaten
⅔	cup currants
1	teaspoon ground cinnamon
4½ to 5	cups all-purpose flour

Icing:

½	cup sifted powdered sugar
¼	teaspoon vanilla
2 to 3	teaspoons milk

◆   ◆   ◆

For four generations, women in Blanche Brobeil Spaulding's family have been making her grandmother's recipe for Hot Cross Buns during Lent. Blanche's children say that memories of their mom's baking are so strong that when they call her from Wichita, New York City and Chicago, they can smell Hot Cross Buns baking in the oven.

Blanche Brobeil Spaulding
The Thresher Table
Bethel College
Women's Association
North Newton
KANSAS

1 Scald the milk. While hot, transfer to a large mixing bowl and add the sugar, shortening and salt. Cool to lukewarm.

2 Dissolve the yeast in the lukewarm water and add to the milk mixture.

3 Add the eggs, currants and cinnamon. Stir in as much flour as you can with a wooden spoon.

4 On a lightly floured surface, knead in enough of the remaining flour to make a moderately soft dough that is smooth and elastic (3 to 5 minutes).

5 Place the dough in a greased bowl and turn once to grease the surface. Cover and let the dough rise until it is doubled in size (about 45 minutes).

6 Punch the dough down. Cover and let the dough rest for 10 minutes more.

7 Divide the dough into 20 portions. Shape into smooth balls. Place the balls 2 to 2½ inches apart onto large greased baking sheets. Cover and let rise until they are nearly doubled in size (about 20 minutes).

8 Preheat oven to 350°. Mark a crisscross on each bun with a sharp knife. Bake in the 350° oven about 20 minutes or until lightly browned. Remove from the baking sheets and cool on wire racks.

9 To make the icing: In a small bowl, stir together the powdered sugar, vanilla and enough milk to make the icing a piping consistency. When the buns are cool, pipe the icing along the crosses on top of the buns.

 TIPS FROM OUR KITCHEN

If you don't have a decorating bag to pipe the icing, make one from a plastic sandwich bag. Place the icing in the bag and force it into one corner. Then cut off a small tip from the corner.

Nutrition Analysis *(Per Bun)*: Calories: 175 / Cholesterol: 22 mg / Carbohydrates: 30 g / Protein: 4 g / Sodium: 67 mg / Fat: 4 g (Saturated Fat: 1 g) / Potassium: 110 mg.

savory breads & pancakes

Few things are as inviting as the aroma of baking bread filling the house—both to the heart and to the tastebuds! Imagine welcoming guests to your home or your family to Sunday brunch with the rich goodness of Vermont Cheddar Cheese Batter Bread. Hearty Sausage Bread is practically a meal unto itself, and intriguing Onion Twist Bread makes an out-of-this-world accompaniment to a variety of dishes. Need a simple yet sublime side? Try Foolproof Popovers, Crispy Cornsticks, or Sour Milk Biscuits. And Golden Zucchini Pancakes or Classic Potato Pancakes provide piquant alternatives to their sweeter cousins.

NORTHERN MAINE OATMEAL BREAD

NORTHERN MAINE OATMEAL BREAD

Makes 2 Loaves (32 Servings)

2	cups boiling water
1	tablespoon butter *or* margarine
1	cup rolled oats
1	package active dry yeast
½	cup warm water (110° to 115°F)
½	cup molasses
2	teaspoons salt
5¾ to 6¼	cups all-purpose flour

Melted butter

◆　　◆　　◆

When Joan moved with her husband from Massachusetts to Maine over 40 years ago, a friend gave her this old Maine recipe to take with her. It's a favorite with family and guests alike, sometimes even outshining the main dish. Joan's friend Millie shapes the dough into rolls, which she claims can transform a turkey sandwich into a gourmet creation.

Mrs. Joan Granger
Merrymeeting Merry Eating
Regional Memorial
Hospital Auxiliary
Brunswick
MAINE

1 In a large mixing bowl, combine the boiling water, butter and rolled oats and let stand for 1 hour (or for 30 minutes if you are using "quick" oats).

2 Dissolve the yeast in the ½ cup warm water. Add the yeast mixture, molasses, salt, and as much flour as you can stir into the oat mixture. Mix thoroughly.

3 On a lightly floured surface, knead the dough for 6 to 8 minutes, adding more flour, if necessary, to form a moderately stiff dough.

4 Place the dough in a greased bowl and turn the dough over once to grease the surface. Cover with a damp cloth and let rise in a warm place until doubled in size (about 45 minutes).

5 Punch the dough down. Divide the dough in half. Cover and let rest for 10 minutes. Shape each portion into a loaf. Place each loaf, seam side down, in a greased 8x4x2-inch or 9x5x3-inch loaf pan and let rise again until almost doubled in size (30 to 40 minutes). Preheat oven to 375°.

6 Bake in the 375° oven about 40 minutes or until bread tests done. Remove the loaves from the pans, brush the tops with melted butter to soften the crusts. Cool the loaves on wire racks.

 TIPS FROM OUR KITCHEN

If you like a rich molasses flavor, use dark molasses rather than light molasses.

There are two ways to shape bread into a basic loaf. One way, shown here, is to roll *each* half of the dough into a 12x8-inch rectangle and roll up tightly, starting at one of the short edges. Another way is to gently pull each half of the dough into a loaf shape and tuck the ends underneath.

For real down-home goodness, slather on the butter and your favorite jam or jelly.

Test for doneness by tapping the loaf with your finger. A hollow sound means the loaf is baked properly.

Nutrition Analysis *(Per Serving)*: Calories: 103 / Cholesterol: 1 mg / Carbohydrates: 21 g / Protein: 3 g / Sodium: 141 mg / Fat: 1 g (Saturated Fat: 0 g) / Potassium: 81 mg.

CHALLAH

Makes 4 Loaves (48 Servings)

2	packages active dry yeast
¾	cup warm water (110° to 115°)
2	teaspoons sugar
½	cup margarine *or* butter
1	cup boiling water
½	cup sugar
¼	cup cooking oil
¼	cup honey
1	tablespoon salt
8	eggs
10	cups all-purpose flour
1	cup raisins
1	egg yolk, beaten
1	teaspoon water
¼	cup poppy seed

◆   ◆   ◆

To raise funds for their Hebrew School, the Sisterhood of Temple Beth-El compiled Cook & Tell, *"the best kosher cookbook ever written." Every year during Chanukah, the Sisterhood has a festival during which they cook and bake all day. This cookbook is a collection of the recipes that were prepared at their festivals.*

Bok Hurwich
Cook & Tell
Sisterhood of Temple Beth-El
Birmingham
ALABAMA

1 In a 1-cup measuring cup, dissolve the yeast in warm water. Stir in the 2 teaspoons sugar and set in a warm place until the mixture rises to the top of the cup.

2 Place the margarine or butter in a large mixing bowl and add the boiling water. After the margarine or butter melts, stir in the ½ cup sugar, cooking oil, honey and salt. Add the eggs, one at a time, beating well with an electric mixer after each addition.

3 Add the yeast mixture to the egg mixture. Beat in *5 cups* of the flour. Stir in *4 cups* of the remaining flour.

4 Turn the dough onto a well-floured board and knead, gradually working in the remaining *1 cup* flour. Shape into a ball and place in a large greased bowl. Cover and let stand in a warm place for 1½ to 2 hours or until doubled in size.

5 Turn the dough out onto a board and knead in the raisins. Divide the dough into 4 portions. Roll each portion into a 30-inch-long rope. Take one rope and hold down one end as you coil the free end of the rope around it counterclockwise to form a round spiral or coil.

6 Place the round spiral loaf on a greased baking sheet. Repeat with the remaining ropes. Cover the loaves and let rise for 1 hour. Preheat the oven to 350°.

7 Stir together the egg yolk with the 1 teaspoon water; brush the mixture over the loaves. Sprinkle the loaves with the poppy seed. Bake in the 350° oven for 35 minutes. If necessary, cover the loaves with foil during the last 15 minutes of baking to prevent over browning.

TIPS FROM OUR KITCHEN

Traditionally, challah is a braided loaf. To make braided loaves: Divide the dough into four equal portions. Then divide each portion into thirds. Roll each into a rope about 14 inches long and place 3 ropes about 1 inch apart on a greased baking sheet. Starting in the middle, braid by bringing the left rope underneath the center rope; lay it down. Then bring the right rope under the new center rope; lay it down. Repeat to the end. Rotate the baking sheet. Beginning once again at the center, braid by bringing the outside ropes alternately over the center rope. Press the rope ends together to seal. Be sure to braid loosely so the bread has room to expand. Repeat with the remaining portions of dough.

Nutrition Analysis (*Per Serving*): Calories: 155 / Cholesterol: 40 mg / Carbohydrates: 25 g / Protein: 4 g / Sodium: 168 mg / Fat: 5 g (Saturated Fat: 1 g) / Potassium: 71 mg.

CHALLAH

OLD-FASHIONED POTATO BREAD

OLD-FASHIONED POTATO BREAD

Makes 2 Loaves (32 Servings)
Packaged instant mashed potatoes

2	packages active dry yeast
2	cups warm water (105° to 115°)
¼	cup sugar
2	teaspoons salt
7½ to 7¾	cups all-purpose flour
½	cup butter *or* margarine, softened
2	tablespoons butter *or* margarine, melted

◆   ◆   ◆

This recipe has probably been in Miriam De Moss's family for sixty years, and Miriam said that it was a favorite of her mother and her grandmother. Miriam often serves Old-Fashioned Potato Bread for Christmas dinner and other special occasions.

Miriam De Moss
Favorite Recipes From
Superstition La Sertoma Club
Superstition La Sertoma Club of Mesa, Arizona
Mesa
ARIZONA

1 Grease two 9x5x3-inch loaf pans; set aside.

2 Make enough instant mashed potatoes for 2 servings *(1 cup)* according to the package directions, using the liquid but omitting the butter or margarine and seasonings.

3 In a large mixing bowl, sprinkle the yeast over the warm water, stirring until the yeast is dissolved. Stir in the sugar and salt until they are dissolved.

4 Add the mashed potatoes, *3½ cups* of the flour and the ½ cup butter or margarine to the yeast mixture. Beat with an electric mixer on medium speed about 2 minutes or until the mixture is smooth. Gradually add *4 cups* of the flour, mixing with your hands until the dough is smooth and stiff enough to leave the sides of the bowl. If necessary, add the remaining flour.

5 Turn out the dough onto a lightly floured surface. Knead the dough for 8 to 10 minutes or until it is smooth and elastic. Place the dough in a large greased bowl, turning the dough once to grease the surface. Cover the bowl with a towel and let the dough rise in a warm place (about 85°) until it is doubled in size (about 1 hour).

6 Turn out the dough onto a lightly floured pastry cloth or surface. Divide the dough in *half.* Roll out each half into a 16x8-inch rectangle. Starting from 1 end, roll up the dough rectangles. Press the ends of the dough rolls until they are even; pinch to seal the dough ends and tuck them under the loaf. Place the loaves, seam side down, in the prepared pans. Brush the tops of the loaves with some of the 2 tablespoons melted butter or margarine.

7 Let the loaves rise in a warm place for 45 minutes to 1 hour or until their tops are rounded. Set the oven rack at the lowest level; preheat the oven to 400°.

8 Bake in the 400° oven for 30 to 35 minutes or until the loaves are golden brown and sound hollow when tapped, making sure that if the crusts brown too quickly during the baking time to loosely cover the tops with aluminum foil.

9 Remove the loaves from the pans and set them on a wire rack. Brush the tops of the loaves with the remaining melted butter or margarine; cool.

 TIPS FROM OUR KITCHEN

A good way to raise the yeast dough is to place the bowl of yeast dough in an unheated oven, then set a large pan of hot water under the bowl on the oven's lower rack.

Nutrition Analysis (*Per Serving*): Calories: 141 / Cholesterol: 10 mg / Carbohydrates: 23 g / Protein: 3 g / Sodium: 173 mg / Fat: 4 g (Saturated Fat: 2 g) / Potassium: 49 mg.

FOOLPROOF POPOVERS

Makes 6 or 8 Large Popovers
- 1   cup all-purpose flour
- 1   cup milk
- 2   eggs
- ½   teaspoon salt

❖   ❖   ❖

In 1953, Dr. June Nichol traveled to New England for an old college friend's wedding. While there, she attended a luncheon hosted by another friend. At the luncheon, June tasted these "spectacular" popovers and immediately asked for the recipe. She began serving Foolproof Popovers at bridge luncheons and to her family. She still serves them often, especially to her children. In fact, although her children are grown, when they come to visit they still ask for June's delicious popovers.

Dr. June Nichol
Southern Accent
The Junior League of Pine Bluff, Inc.
Pine Bluff
ARKANSAS

1 Grease 6 or 8 iron popover pan cups or 6 custard cups. Place the custard cups on a 15x10x1-inch baking pan. Place the popover pan or custard cups in the refrigerator to chill.

2 In a medium mixing bowl, using a wooden spoon, stir together the flour, milk, eggs and salt, until the flour is moist (batter will be lumpy).

3 Pour the batter into the prepared cold popover pan cups or custard cups so that each cup is just under ½-full.

4 Place the popover pan or custard cups into a cold oven and set the temperature to 400°. Bake for 30 to 35 minutes or until the popovers are golden and firm. *Do not open the oven door before 30 minutes have passed.* Remove the popovers from the cups and serve hot.

 TIPS FROM OUR KITCHEN

To help keep these popovers foolproof, use large eggs and measure carefully. Before measuring, stir the flour in the canister to lighten it. Gently spoon the flour into a 1-cup dry measure and level off the top with a metal spatula or knife.

Use nonstick spray coating or about ½ teaspoon *shortening* to grease *each* popover pan cup or custard cup.

If you prick the popovers with a fork after removing them from the oven, they'll be less likely to become soggy. For especially crisp popovers, return the pricked popovers to the oven for 5 to 10 minutes.

The ideal popover is golden and firm. Final baking time will depend on your oven. In some ovens, the popovers may take up to 5 minutes longer to cook. Unless you know your oven is much hotter than normal, *do not* open the oven door before 30 minutes have passed; the cool air might cause the popovers to fall.

Nutrition Analysis *(Per Serving)*: Calories: 124 / Cholesterol: 74 mg / Carbohydrates: 17 g / Protein: 5 g / Sodium: 219 mg / Fat: 4 g (Saturated Fat: 1 g) / Potassium: 103 mg.

FOOLPROOF POPOVERS

CRISPY CORNSTICKS

CRISPY CORNSTICKS

Makes 14 Cornsticks

1	cup yellow cornmeal
½	cup all-purpose flour
2½	teaspoons baking powder
1	teaspoon sugar
½	teaspoon salt
⅛	teaspoon baking soda
2	eggs
1	cup buttermilk
2	tablespoons cooking oil

◆   ◆   ◆

If you grew up in the South, muffins, biscuits, corn bread and cornsticks were a part of your everyday meal. Frances Jolley Syfan said that she makes her Crispy Cornsticks the old southern way—in a hot cornstick pan—"preheating the cornstick pan gives you more of a crispy crust, with a tender inside." She also said that when she has soup, it's just not complete unless she has Crispy Cornsticks with it.

Frances Jolley Syfan
Perennials: A Southern Celebration of Foods and Flavors
The Junior Service League of Gainesville, Georgia
Gainesville
GEORGIA

1 Preheat the oven to 450°. Heavily grease cornstick pans and place them in the oven to heat.

2 Meanwhile, in a medium bowl, stir together the cornmeal, flour, baking powder, sugar, salt and baking soda. Make a well in the center; set aside.

3 In a small bowl, mix together the eggs, buttermilk and cooking oil. Add the egg mixture to the dry ingredients all at once. Stir by hand just until smooth.

4 Transfer the mixture to a large sturdy plastic bag. Cut off one corner. Carefully squeeze the mixture into the hot cornstick pans.

5 Bake in the 450° for 10 to 12 minutes or until the cornsticks are golden.

 TIPS FROM OUR KITCHEN

For corn bread, you can bake this batter in a 9-inch square pan; bake in a 450° oven for 25 minutes.

To reheat the cornsticks: Place them on a plate and cover with paper towels. Micro-cook on 100% power (high) for 15 seconds for 2 cornsticks, or for 20 to 25 seconds for 4 cornsticks.

This recipe also can be baked in shaped iron bakeware pans to make cactus, fish, hearts or other shapes. Follow the directions provided for using the pan.

Nutrition Analysis (*Per Cornstick*): Calories: 88 / Cholesterol: 31 mg / Carbohydrates: 12 g / Protein: 3 g / Sodium: 117 mg / Fat: 3 g (Saturated Fat: 1 g) / Potassium: 57 mg.

FIESTA CORN BREAD

Makes 8 or 9 Servings
- 1 cup all-purpose flour
- 1 cup yellow cornmeal
- 1 tablespoon baking powder
- ½ teaspoon salt
- 2 eggs, beaten
- ⅔ cup milk
- ¼ cup melted shortening *or* cooking oil
- 1½ cups shredded sharp cheddar cheese (6 ounces)
- 1 8-ounce can cream-style corn
- 1 4-ounce can chopped hot *or* mild green chilies, drained

❖ ❖ ❖

Finding and trying new recipes is one of Myrtle Nowell's hobbies. She found this family favorite many years ago and adjusts the degree of hotness by varying the strength of the chilies she uses.

Myrtle Nowell
Thank Heaven for Homemade
Cooks Cookbook
Dewitt Nursing Home
Dewitt
ARIZONA

1 Preheat oven to 400°.

2 In a medium mixing bowl, stir together the flour, cornmeal, baking powder and salt. Set aside.

3 In another bowl, beat together the eggs, milk and melted shortening or cooking oil. Add to the flour mixture and stir just until the batter is smooth.

4 Fold in the cheddar cheese, cream-style corn and green chilies.

5 Spread the mixture in a greased 9x9x2-inch baking pan or a 9-inch cast-iron skillet. Bake in the 400° oven for 30 to 35 minutes or until golden brown and a wooden toothpick inserted near the center comes out clean.

 TIPS FROM OUR KITCHEN

To give this corn bread a unique shape, bake it in a cast-iron skillet that measures 9 inches across the bottom. Then cut it into wedges to serve.

For a really fiery bread, substitute pepper cheese for the cheddar cheese. Then serve the corn bread with grilled, broiled or baked meat or poultry.

Nutrition Analysis (*Per Serving*): Calories: 310 / Cholesterol: 77 mg / Carbohydrates: 32 g / Protein: 11 g / Sodium: 547 mg / Fat: 16 g (Saturated Fat: 7 g) / Potassium: 161 mg.

FIESTA CORN BREAD

VERMONT CHEDDAR CHEESE BATTER BREAD

VERMONT CHEDDAR CHEESE BATTER BREAD

Makes 1 Loaf (16 Servings)

- 1 package active dry yeast
- 1¼ cups warm water (105° to 115°)
- 2⅔ cups all-purpose flour
- 1 cup shredded sharp Vermont cheddar cheese (4 ounces)
- 2 tablespoons sugar
- 2 tablespoons shortening
- 1 teaspoon salt
- 1 teaspoon melted butter *or* margarine

❖ ❖ ❖

The Elizabeth H. Brown Humane Society provides animal care services including assisting in the placement of abandoned or unwanted animals. Deborah Hart's recipe for Vermont Cheddar Cheese Batter Bread comes to us from the society's fund-raising cookbook. Deborah tells us that she found a recipe for a cheese bread years ago and made little changes here and there to make it more her own. Delicious!

Deborah Hart
Elizabeth H. Brown Humane
Society Cookbook
Elizabeth H. Brown
Humane Society
Barton
VERMONT

1 In a large mixing bowl, dissolve the yeast in the warm water. Add *1⅔ cups* of the flour, the cheese, sugar, shortening and salt. Beat with an electric mixer on low speed for 30 seconds, scraping the bowl as needed. Beat on medium speed for 2 minutes, continuing to scrape the bowl.

2 Add the remaining *1 cup* flour, stirring until combined and scraping the batter from the sides of the bowl. Cover and let rise in a warm place for 30 minutes. Then, stir about 25 strokes.

3 Spread the batter evenly in a greased 1½-quart glass casserole. Cover and let rise in warm place about 45 minutes or until the batter has doubled in size.

4 Preheat the oven to 375°. Bake in the 375° oven for 40 to 45 minutes or until golden brown. Cover with foil the last 25 minutes of baking to prevent the top from overbrowning.

5 Remove the bread from the oven and brush the top with the melted butter or margarine. Remove the bread from the pan and cool on a wire rack.

 TIPS FROM OUR KITCHEN

This bread also can be baked in a greased 9x5x3-inch loaf pan or in two greased 7½x3½x2-inch loaf pans.

No-knead breads such as this batter bread generally have a more open, coarse texture than do kneaded breads.

If Vermont cheddar cheese is not sold in your area, feel free to substitute any variety of sharp cheddar cheese.

Nutrition Analysis *(Per Serving)*: Calories: 121 / Cholesterol: 8 mg / Carbohydrates: 16 g / Protein: 4 g / Sodium: 181 mg / Fat: 4 g (Saturated Fat: 2 g) / Potassium: 36 mg.

SOUR MILK BISCUITS

Makes 24 Biscuits
4¼ cups all-purpose flour
1 tablespoon plus 1 teaspoon baking powder
1 teaspoon baking soda
¾ teaspoon salt
½ cup shortening
2 cups sour milk *or* buttermilk

❖ ❖ ❖

Back in 1819, the small town of Etna, New Hampshire, gathered for its very first community Chicken Pie Supper. Grandma Derby made her famous chicken pie and Bertha LaBombard contributed her light, flaky Sour Milk Biscuits—and the town had a bona fide annual hit on its hands. Rumor has it that people came from miles around—by horse and buggy, no less—just to get a taste. Today, 219,000 suppers later, Etna still gathers for their Chicken Pie Suppers, raising funds for their community and satisfying hungry townsfolk in one grand feast.

Bertha LaBombard
<u>Hanover Center Cooks</u>
Etna
NEW HAMPSHIRE

1 Preheat oven to 400°. Lightly grease 2 baking sheets. Or, for soft-sided biscuits, lightly grease 2 round baking pans.

2 In a large bowl, stir together the flour, baking powder, baking soda and salt. Using a pastry blender or 2 knives, cut in the shortening until the mixture resembles coarse crumbs. Gradually stir in the sour milk or buttermilk until a soft dough forms.

3 Turn the dough out onto a lightly floured surface. Gently knead the dough for 10 to 12 strokes.

4 On a lightly floured surface, pat or roll the dough out to a ½-inch thickness. If necessary, add a little flour to the surface of the dough or rolling pin to keep the dough from sticking.

5 Using a 2½-inch biscuit cutter, cut out as many dough rounds as possible. Dip the biscuit cutter into flour between cuts to help prevent sticking. Press the cutter straight down to get straight-sided biscuits. Do not twist the cutter or flatten the biscuit edges.

6 Carefully transfer the cut biscuits to the prepared baking sheets or baking pans. For crusty-sided biscuits, place the rounds about 1 inch apart on the baking sheets. For soft-sided biscuits, place the rounds close together in the pans.

7 Bake in the 400° oven about 15 minutes or until the biscuits are puffed and golden. Serve the biscuits warm.

 TIPS FROM OUR KITCHEN

To make sour milk: In a 2-cup glass measure, place 2 tablespoons vinegar. Add enough milk to make 2 cups. Let the milk mixture stand at room temperature for 5 minutes before using.

Nutrition Analysis (*Per Biscuit*): Calories: 117 / Cholesterol: 1 mg / Carbohydrates: 16 g / Protein: 3 g / Sodium: 177 mg / Fat: 5 g (Saturated Fat: 1 g) / Potassium: 52 mg.

SOUR MILK BISCUITS

SPOON BREAD

SPOON BREAD

Makes 6 to 8 Servings

1 cup cornmeal
3 cups milk
2 tablespoons shortening
1 teaspoon baking powder
1 teaspoon salt
3 egg yolks, beaten
3 egg whites

◆ ◆ ◆

Although Agnes Pearcy had never heard of Spoon Bread when she tried it for the first time at a luncheon in Oklahoma City in 1947, Spoon Bread was already an established favorite dish in that area. Since then, she has served it to many a skeptical friend—several who had not heard of Spoon Bread either—and always with success. Agnes suggests serving this bread with chicken, in place of potatoes or rice. We predict that your guests will return for seconds and thirds.

Agnes M. Pearcy
Charity's Cherished Recipes
DePaul Health Center
Auxiliary
Bridgeton
MISSOURI

1 Preheat the oven to 350°. Grease a 2-quart square baking dish. Set aside.

2 In a medium mixing bowl, stir together the cornmeal and *1 cup* of the milk.

3 In a 2-quart saucepan, over medium heat, warm the remaining 2 cups milk. Slowly stir the cornmeal mixture into the hot milk. Reduce the heat to low and cook, stirring frequently, for 10 minutes (mixture will be thick). Remove from heat.

4 In a clean, medium mixing bowl using an electric mixer, beat the egg whites until they hold stiff peaks (tips stand straight). Set aside.

5 Stir the shortening, baking powder and salt into the cornmeal-milk mixture. Stir in the beaten egg yolks. Fold in the beaten egg whites.

6 Turn the mixture into the prepared baking dish. Bake, uncovered, in the 350° oven for 40 to 45 minutes or until a knife inserted into the center comes out clean. Serve hot.

 TIPS FROM OUR KITCHEN

It is necessary to stir the cornmeal-milk mixture frequently while it is cooking so that it thickens uniformly. Cook over low heat and be aware that the mixture will "pop" occasionally.

For variety, add 2 tablespoons sliced green onion or chopped green chili peppers, or ½ cup grated Parmesan cheese to the Spoon Bread batter.

For a boost in flavor, use margarine or butter in place of the shortening.

Nutrition Analysis (*Per Serving*): Calories: 227 / Cholesterol: 116 mg / Carbohydrates: 24 g / Protein: 9 g / Sodium: 503 mg / Fat: 10 g (Saturated Fat: 3 g) / Potassium: 257 mg.

ONION TWIST BREAD

Makes 1 Loaf (16 Servings)

  1 package active dry yeast
 ¼ cup warm water (105° to 115°)
4 to 4½ cups all-purpose flour
 ½ cup melted margarine *or* butter
 ½ cup milk
 ½ cup hot water (120° to 130°)
 ¼ cup sugar
  1 egg, beaten
1½ teaspoons salt

Filling:
  1 cup finely chopped onion
 ¼ cup margarine *or* butter
  1 tablespoon grated Parmesan cheese
  1 tablespoon sesame seed
  1 tablespoon poppy seed
 ¼ teaspoon garlic salt
  1 teaspoon paprika

◆   ◆   ◆

Debi says she doesn't often have the chance to give Onion Twist Bread loaves as gifts. "Everyone smells the bread baking and waits for it to come out of the oven. When it's cool enough to cut, it's half gone!"

Debi Maas
The Dollar a Month Club
Anniversary Cookbook: A
Collection of Recipes to
Celebrate the Year
Jesuit Jamshedpur Mission
Baltimore
MARYLAND

1 To make the dough: In a mixing bowl, stir yeast into the warm water. Let the mixture stand for 10 minutes.

2 Stir in *2 cups* of the flour, the melted margarine or butter, milk, hot water, sugar, beaten egg and salt. Beat with an electric mixer on low speed until moistened; beat for 2 minutes more on medium speed. Stir in *2 cups* additional flour.

3 On a floured surface, knead in enough of the remaining flour to make a moderately stiff dough (5 to 8 minutes). Place in a greased bowl. Turn the dough once to grease the surface. Cover and let rise in a warm place until doubled in size, about 1 hour.

4 To make the filling: Cook and stir the onion in the ¼ cup margarine or butter until the onion is tender but not brown. Stir in Parmesan cheese, sesame and poppy seeds, garlic salt and paprika. Set aside.

5 Punch down the dough. If necessary, coat the dough lightly with flour until it is no longer sticky. Roll the dough into a 16x9-inch rectangle. Cut it lengthwise into 3 strips, each 16x4 inches.

6 Spread the filling down the center of each strip. Pull the dough up and around the filling. Carefully seal the edges and ends and transfer the filled strips to a greased baking sheet, placing them about 1 inch apart. (Because this a long loaf, place the strips diagonally on the baking sheet.)

7 Gently pull the strips, stretching until each measures about 18 inches in length. Starting in the middle, loosely braid by bringing the left strip underneath the center strip; lay it down. Then bring the right strip under the new center strip; lay it down. Repeat to the end, keeping the seams inside the braid when possible. Press the ends together.

8 On the other end, loosely braid from the middle of the loaf by bringing the outside strips alternately over the center strip. Press the ends together.

9 Cover and let the braid rise in a warm place until nearly doubled in size. Preheat the oven to 350°. Bake in the 350° oven about 40 minutes or until golden brown.

Nutrition Analysis (*Per Serving*): Calories: 266 / Cholesterol: 14 mg / Carbohydrates: 27 g / Protein: 5 g / Sodium: 416 mg / Fat: 16 g (Saturated Fat: 3 g) / Potassium: 89 mg.

ONION TWIST BREAD

SAUSAGE BREAD

SAUSAGE BREAD

Makes 1 Loaf (8 Slices)

1	pound bulk Italian sausage
1	pound loaf frozen bread dough, thawed
1	egg, slightly beaten
2	tablespoons snipped parsley
1	tablespoon snipped fresh basil *or* 1 teaspoon dried basil, crushed
1	cup shredded mozzarella cheese
1 to 2	tablespoons olive oil

◆　　◆　　◆

Somewhere, sometime, we've all tasted a dish we loved so much we just had to have the recipe. That's what happened when Marsha Paulsell tasted this Sausage Bread at her neighbor's house. The neighbor kindly gave the recipe to Marsha, who began serving the bread to her family, friends and children's friends. The demand for this popular bread spread throughout the entire Overlake School. So when the school decided to create a fund-raising cookbook, naturally this recipe was considered a must.

Marsha Paulsell
The Overlake School Cookbook
Redmond
WASHINGTON

1 Preheat oven to 375°. Lightly grease a baking sheet.

2 In a large skillet, cook and stir the sausage for 8 to 10 minutes or until it is browned. Drain off the excess fat.

3 Pat the bread dough into a 12x9-inch rectangle on the prepared baking sheet. Combine the sausage with the egg, parsley and basil.

4 Spread the sausage filling evenly over the dough rectangle, leaving a 1½-inch border. Sprinkle the mozzarella cheese over the filling.

5 Starting at a short side, roll up the dough jelly-roll fashion. Tuck under the ends and place the loaf, seam side down, in the center of the baking sheet. Brush the loaf lightly with the olive oil.

6 Bake the loaf in the 375° oven about 30 minutes or until it is light brown and sounds hollow when tapped on the bottom. Cool the loaf slightly on a wire rack. Serve the bread warm.

TIPS FROM OUR KITCHEN

To seal the ends of the loaf, after rolling up the dough rectangle, press down on each end to make a thin sealed strip. Then fold the strips under the loaf.

To make Sausage Bread a complete meal, serve it with your favorite soup or a chef's salad.

For a zesty appetizer, slice the baked loaf into 16 slices. Then cut each slice in half crosswise. Serve the slices on a platter with a small bowl of mustard for dipping.

Nutrition Analysis (*Per Slice*): Calories: 329 / Cholesterol: 67 mg / Carbohydrates: 26 g / Protein: 17 g / Sodium: 483 mg / Fat: 17 g (Saturated Fat: 6 g) / Potassium: 209 mg.

GOLDEN ZUCCHINI PANCAKES

Makes 12 Pancakes

 3 medium zucchini, shredded
   (4 cups)
 ½ teaspoon salt
 ½ cup finely chopped onion
 1 tablespoon butter *or*
   margarine
 2 eggs, slightly beaten
 ¼ cup all-purpose flour
 ⅛ teaspoon pepper
Cooking oil

◆　◆　◆

*When Nancy Griffin's organic
gardener friends share their
harvest, Golden Zucchini
Pancakes are likely to appear on
—and disappear from—Nancy's
dining table. She says that her
family likes them best served with
tomato sauce as a side dish.*

Nancy Griffin
<u>*Happiness is Anything*</u>
<u>*Homemade*</u>
*Worcester Area Association for
Retarded Citizens, Inc.
Worcester
MASSACHUSETTS*

1 Place the zucchini in a colander.
Sprinkle with salt and set aside for 30
minutes.

2 Squeeze as much of the liquid as
possible from the zucchini with your
hands.

3 In a medium skillet, cook the onions
in the butter or margarine over medium heat about 3 minutes or until
tender, stirring occasionally.

4 Transfer the zucchini and onions to a
large bowl. Stir in the eggs, flour and
pepper.

5 Pour the cooking oil into a clean
medium skillet to a depth of ⅛ inch.
Heat over medium-high heat.

6 Drop slightly rounded tablespoons
of the batter into the hot oil and flatten
to 3-inch diameters with the back of
a spoon.

7 Cook the pancakes over medium-
high heat until golden, turning once (2
to 3 minutes on each side). Remove the
pancakes with a slotted spatula and
drain on paper towels. Add more oil to
the skillet, if needed, and repeat until
all of the batter is used.

 TIPS FROM OUR KITCHEN

When yellow summer squash is
plentiful, substitute it for the zucchini.

Dress up these pancakes by adding ¼
cup shredded carrot to the batter.

If you like, drizzle the pancakes with
your favorite cheese sauce.

Nutrition Analysis *(Per Pancake)*: Calories: 80 / Cholesterol: 36 mg / Carbohydrates: 4 g /
Protein: 2 g / Sodium: 67 mg / Fat: 6 g (Saturated Fat: 1 g) / Potassium: 96 mg.

GOLDEN ZUCCHINI PANCAKES

CLASSIC POTATO PANCAKES

CLASSIC POTATO PANCAKES

Makes 10 Pancakes

1	pound potatoes, peeled
2	eggs, lightly beaten
¼	cup finely chopped onion
1	teaspoon salt
¼	teaspoon pepper
2 to 4	tablespoons matzoh meal *or* finely crushed saltine crackers
2	tablespoons cooking oil

Dairy sour cream, applesauce *and/or* cinnamon-sugar

❖   ❖   ❖

The recipe for Classic Potato Pancakes is just one of the many delicious inclusions in the Stanford University Medical Center Auxiliary Cookbook. Cookbook Chairperson Molly Huckins told us that the contributor of these tasty concoctions, Joe Carcione, was a very well-known speaker in the San Francisco Bay Area. Known as the "Green Grocer," he often appeared on television to share his wonderful repertoire of recipes.

Joe Carcione
<u>Stanford University Medical</u>
<u>Center Auxiliary Cookbook</u>
Stanford University Medical
Center Auxiliary
Stanford
CALIFORNIA

1 Coarsely shred the potatoes into a large bowl of *cold water*; drain well.

2 In another large bowl, stir together the lightly beaten eggs, onion, salt, pepper and shredded potatoes. Stir in enough of the matzoh meal or crushed saltine crackers to make a thick batter.

3 In a 10-inch skillet or on a griddle over medium-high heat, heat the cooking oil until hot. Using about ¼ *cup* of the batter for *each* pancake, spoon the batter into the hot cooking oil, leaving about ½ inch between each pancake. Cook the pancakes about 5 minutes on each side or until the pancakes are crisp and brown on both sides. Transfer the pancakes to paper towels; drain and keep warm. Repeat with the remaining batter.

4 Serve the potato pancakes while they are hot with the sour cream, applesauce and/or cinnamon-sugar on the side.

TIPS FROM OUR KITCHEN

Shredding the potatoes directly into a bowl of cold water prevents them from discoloring. You may want to use a hand shredder rather than a food processor in order to quickly shred the potatoes into the water. If you use a food processor, however, put the shredded potato into a bowl of cold water immediately after shredding it.

Check how hot the cooking oil is by dropping a drop or two of water on the hot skillet or griddle. The water droplets will "dance" when the skillet is hot enough to cook the pancakes. Carefully watch the cooking temperature after adding the batter because if the heat is too high, the surface of the pancake will brown before the insides are cooked through.

Matzoh meal is crumbled matzoh—the large flat sheets of unleavened bread that are usually made with only flour and water. Look for matzoh meal in the specialty food section of your supermarket.

Nutrition Analysis (*Per Pancake*): Calories: 98 / Cholesterol: 45 mg / Carbohydrates: 11 g / Protein: 2 g / Sodium: 231 mg / Fat: 5 g (Saturated Fat: 1 g) / Potassium: 177 mg.

chapter three

sandwiches
& savory pies

Feast your eyes on this lunchtime (or brunchtime!) extravaganza of scrumptious sandwiches and rib-sticking main-dish pies. You'll find something for every occasion, from the exquisite Austrian Cheese and Shrimp Strudel—perfect for a bridal or baby shower—to zesty Brunch Sausage Casserole—a natural for the Sunday afternoon football crowd. Familiar favorites, such as Monte Cristo Sandwiches and Noodle Kugel, stand side-by-side with creative newcomers, such as Vagabond Pies or Showhouse Sun-Up Rice. Whether you make one large dish or make several and serve a tasty array of appetizer-sized portions, your family and friends will leave you no leftovers.

TUNA AND CHEESE SANDWICH

TUNA AND CHEESE SANDWICH

Makes 4 Servings

1	tablespoon cooking oil
1	cup chopped apple
3	tablespoons finely chopped onion
1	7-ounce can water-packed tuna, drained
¼	cup finely chopped walnuts
¼	cup mayonnaise *or* salad dressing
2	teaspoons lemon juice
⅛	teaspoon salt
⅛	teaspoon pepper
4	slices raisin bread, toasted
4	slices sharp cheddar cheese (3 ounces)

❖   ❖   ❖

Like many of us, Deborah Mulvey is a busy woman who needs a repertoire of fast and interesting meals that can be made from what's in the house. Since apples and cheese are abundant in Vermont and canned tuna is usually on the shelf, they naturally came to mind and hand when Deborah created this filling for a warm, weekend sandwich.

Deborah Mulvey
Elizabeth H. Brown Humane
Society Cookbook
Elizabeth H. Brown Humane
Society
St. Johnsbury
VERMONT

1 Heat the oil in a small skillet. Add the apple and onion and cook, stirring occasionally, about 5 minutes or until tender.

2 In a medium bowl, stir together the apple-onion mixture, tuna, walnuts, mayonnaise, lemon juice, salt and pepper.

3 Place the 4 slices of toast on a baking sheet and top each one with the tuna mixture and a slice of cheese. Broil 4 to 5 inches from the heat for 3 to 4 minutes or until the cheese is melted.

 TIPS FROM OUR KITCHEN

Next time, try this tuna filling on rye or whole wheat bread or on English muffins. It's delicious!

For a fancy presentation, cut each slice of cheese in half diagonally. Place cheese triangles on top of the tuna before broiling.

Fresh fruit such as grapes and kiwi fruit makes a perfect accompaniment to these savory sandwiches.

Nutrition Analysis *(Per Serving)*: Calories: 420 / Cholesterol: 51 mg / Carbohydrates: 20 g / Protein: 22 g / Sodium: 566 mg / Fat: 28 g (Saturated Fat: 8 g) / Potassium: 311 mg.

TUNA SANDWICH CASSEROLE

Makes 6 to 8 Servings

12	slices bread
3	tablespoons margarine *or* butter, softened
2	6⅛-ounce cans tuna, drained and flaked
1½	cups chopped celery
¾	cup chopped green sweet pepper
½	cup chopped onion (about 1 medium)
¾	cup mayonnaise *or* salad dressing
4	eggs
2	cups milk
1	10¾-ounce can condensed cream of mushroom soup

♦　　♦　　♦

Terry Home, Inc. is currently in the developmental stages of creating a home to provide care for young adults with head injuries. A committee has been formed to raise money through dinners, dances, car shows and the cookbook, <u>Food & Fun</u>. Plans for the building have been prepared, and so far the committee has raised $50,000 toward the purchase of the property.

Ethel Wilson
<u>*Terry Home Presents Food & Fun From Celebrities & Us*</u>
Terry Home, Inc.
Auburn
WASHINGTON

1 Grease a 3-quart rectangular baking dish; set aside.

2 Trim the crusts from the bread slices. Spread a side of *6* of the bread slices with *half* of the softened butter or margarine. Place the bread slices, buttered side up, over the bottom of the prepared baking dish, trimming the bread slices as necessary to fit; set aside.

3 In a large bowl, stir together the tuna, celery, green sweet pepper and onion. Add the mayonnaise or salad dressing; stir to combine all of the ingredients.

4 Spread the tuna mixture over the buttered bread slices in the baking dish. Spread the remaining margarine or butter over a side of *each* of the remaining bread slices. Place the bread slices, buttered side up, over the tuna mixture, trimming the slices as necessary to fit.

5 In a large bowl using a wire whisk, beat the eggs. Stir in the milk and un-diluted cream of mushroom soup; mix well. Carefully pour the soup mixture evenly over the bread and tuna layers in the baking dish. Cover the baking dish and chill in the refrigerator overnight.

6 Preheat the oven to 350°. Bake the casserole, uncovered, in the 350° oven about 1 hour or until the top of the casserole is golden brown.

 TIPS FROM OUR KITCHEN

Whole wheat, rye or white bread work well in this recipe.

Other canned meats, such as chicken and salmon, can be substituted for the tuna in this recipe.

For a little added flavor, substitute 2 tablespoons of pickle relish for part of the chopped green sweet pepper. Or, add ½ teaspoon of dried dillweed to the soup mixture.

Nutrition Analysis (*Per Serving*): Calories: 626 / Cholesterol: 188 mg / Carbohydrates: 38 g / Protein: 28 g / Sodium: 1236 mg / Fat: 40 g (Saturated Fat: 8 g) / Potassium: 590 mg.

TUNA SANDWICH CASSEROLE

AUSTRIAN CHEESE AND SHRIMP STRUDEL

AUSTRIAN CHEESE AND SHRIMP STRUDEL

Makes 16 to 18 Slices

½ 17¼-ounce package (1 sheet) frozen puff pastry, thawed

1½ cups shredded Swiss cheese (6 ounces)

½ cup dairy sour cream

¼ cup thinly sliced green onion

4 ounces cooked shrimp (1 cup), chopped *or* one 4½-ounce can shrimp, rinsed, drained and chopped

1 egg, beaten

◆   ◆   ◆

Lori Stenglein has quite a recipe collection. When traveling, she enjoys collecting regional community cookbooks and recipe clippings from magazines and newspapers. Lori said that if she doesn't use a recipe within a year, she discards it. This recipe for Austrian Cheese and Shrimp Strudel has endured, perhaps because of its simplicity; according to Lori, "This is from my easier and faster category."

Lori Stenglein
The Flavor & Spice
of Holy Cross Life
Holy Cross Parish
Batavia
ILLINOIS

1 Preheat the oven to 400°. On a lightly floured surface, roll the thawed puff pastry to an 18x10-inch rectangle.

2 In a medium bowl, stir together the Swiss cheese, sour cream, green onion, shrimp and *half* of the beaten egg (about 2 tablespoons). Spread the mixture lengthwise down half of the rectangle. Using a pastry brush, brush the edges of the pastry with some of the remaining beaten egg.

3 Carefully fold the dough over the filling and seal the edges with the tines of a fork. Transfer the strudel to an extra large baking sheet. Brush the top and sides of the strudel with the remaining beaten egg.

4 Bake in the 400° oven for 20 to 25 minutes or until golden. Remove from the oven. Cool the strudel for 20 minutes before slicing.

TIPS FROM OUR KITCHEN

If your grocer doesn't have puff pastry in sheets, buy frozen patty shells. When thawed, they, too, can be pressed together and rolled flat to make a sheet.

Brushing the edges of the pastry with the beaten egg helps them to seal and thus reduces the chances of the filling leaking out during baking. Brushing the egg over the strudel helps it to turn a golden brown during baking.

Be sure to let the strudel cool for 20 minutes before slicing. This will give the cheesy filling a chance to set up.

Nutrition Analysis (*Per Slice*): Calories: 134 / Cholesterol: 40 mg / Carbohydrates: 6 g / Protein: 6 g / Sodium: 109 mg / Fat: 10 g (Saturated Fat: 3 g) / Potassium: 40 mg.

COLD HAM AND CHEESE CREPES

Makes 24 Appetizers

Crepe Batter:
- ½ cup cold milk
- ½ cup cold water
- 2 eggs
- 2½ tablespoons butter *or* margarine, melted and cooled
- ¼ teaspoon salt
- ¾ cup all-purpose flour

Filling:
- ½ cup ham, minced
- ½ cup Swiss cheese, shredded
- 1 egg, hard-cooked and coarsely chopped
- ¼ cup finely chopped celery
- 1 tablespoon snipped parsley
- 1 teaspoon sweet pickle relish
- 2 tablespoons mayonnaise
- ¼ teaspoon salt
- ⅛ teaspoon pepper

Sauce:
- ¼ cup dairy sour cream
- ¼ cup mayonnaise
- ¼ teaspoon lemon juice
- 1½ teaspoons snipped parsley
- ½ teaspoon Dijon-style mustard
- Parsley

◆　　◆　　◆

Nancy Parker operated a cooking school for fifteen years. These wonderful crepes were developed for use in class demonstrations.

From the files of Nancy Parker's Cooking School
Cook's Collage
The Junior League of Tulsa, Inc.
Tulsa
OKLAHOMA

1 To make the crepes: In a blender container, combine the milk, water, eggs, butter or margarine and salt. Cover and blend well. Add the flour and blend for 1 minute. Stop the blender and use a spatula to scrape the flour on the sides of the container into the batter. Blend again.

2 Lightly grease a 6-inch skillet by brushing with cooking oil or shortening. Heat over medium heat until a bead of water dropped on the surface sizzles. Pour in about *2 tablespoons* of the crepe batter, then lift and tilt the skillet to spread the batter. Return the skillet to the heat and cook the crepe on one side only for 45 to 60 seconds, or until it is lightly browned on the bottom. Loosen the crepe by running a small metal spatula around the edges. Carefully invert the pan over paper toweling and remove the crepe. Repeat with the remaining batter, greasing the skillet as needed. Set aside 6 crepes. Wrap and freeze the remaining crepes for another use.

3 To make the filling: In a medium bowl, stir together the ham, cheese, egg, celery, parsley and relish. Mix well. Stir in the mayonnaise, salt and pepper. Refrigerate until ready to assemble the appetizers.

4 To assemble: Divide the ham and cheese filling among the 6 crepes and spread it down the center of each with a spoon. Roll each crepe, then cut into fourths.

5 To make the sauce: In a small bowl, stir together the sour cream, mayonnaise, lemon juice, parsley and Dijon-style mustard. Mix well. Refrigerate until ready to serve.

6 To serve: Place the quartered crepes on a serving dish and, if desired, spoon sauce over each. Alternatively, serve the sauce on the side for dipping. Garnish with parsley.

 TIPS FROM OUR KITCHEN

If the crepe batter sticks to a properly seasoned pan, you may need to use higher heat. If the batter won't swirl to coat, it is probably too thick; thin it by gradually stirring in a little milk. If the pan is too hot, the batter may not swirl to coat. Try reducing the temperature.

Nutrition Analysis *(Per Serving)*: Calories: 79 / Cholesterol: 36 mg / Carbohydrates: 4 g / Protein: 3 g / Sodium: 133 mg / Fat: 6 g (Saturated Fat: 2 g) / Potassium: 42 mg.

COLD HAM AND CHEESE CREPES

STROMBOLI

STROMBOLI

Makes 12 Main-Dish Servings

- 2   1-pound loaves frozen bread dough, thawed
- 2   tablespoons Dijon-style mustard
- 8   ounces Genoa salami, thinly sliced
- 8   ounces provolone cheese, thinly sliced
- 8   ounces ham, thinly sliced
- 8   ounces mozzarella cheese, thinly sliced
- 8   ounces fresh bulk pork *or* Italian sausage, cooked, drained and crumbled
- ¼   cup butter *or* margarine, melted
- ¼   cup grated Parmesan cheese
- 1   teaspoon dried oregano, crushed
- ½   teaspoon garlic powder

◆   ◆   ◆

The Junior League of Gaston County hosts many projects for children, including Kids on the Block and Kids Count. Kids on the Block is a puppet program, using "disabled and nondisabled puppets . . . as an educational tool in the elementary schools," and Kids Count is a health and information fair available to parents and youth in the county.

Lynda Nelson
Southern Elegance
Junior League of Gaston County
Gastonia
NORTH CAROLINA

1 On a lightly floured surface, roll *each* portion of the thawed bread dough into a 16x10-inch rectangle. (If desired, cut each rectangle in *half* to make 4 loaves.) Spread *1 tablespoon* of the Dijon-style mustard down the middle of *each* dough rectangle.

2 Divide the Genoa salami, provolone cheese, ham and mozzarella cheese equally and layer each ingredient down the center of *each* dough rectangle. Sprinkle the crumbled sausage down the centers of the dough rectangles.

3 Fold both sides of *each* dough rectangle to the center. Moisten the dough edges and pinch together to seal. Seal the ends of the dough and tuck under.

4 Preheat the oven to 350°. Place the loaves on a greased baking sheet, seam side down. Brush the tops of the loaves with the melted butter or margarine. Sprinkle the top of each loaf with the grated Parmesan cheese, oregano, garlic powder and a dash *pepper*. Bake immediately or let the loaves rise in a warm place for 40 to 50 minutes or until nearly doubled in size. Bake the loaves in the 350° oven for 25 minutes.

TIPS FROM OUR KITCHEN

If you are planning to use frozen bread dough, be sure to allow enough time for the dough to thaw and thaw it according to the package directions. You can also experiment with whole wheat dough as well as the white variety.

These sandwich loaves are perfect for a picnic or tailgate party. If you prefer hot sandwiches, bake the Stromboli just before leaving for the picnic. Cut the loaves into serving sizes, wrap each serving in a double layer of aluminum foil and place the individual servings in an insulated bag that's been warmed with hot water. For cold sandwiches, prepare and bake the loaves the night before and chill them in the refrigerator. Cut the loaves into serving portions and wrap each serving individually.

Nutrition Analysis (*Per Serving*): Calories: 468 / Cholesterol: 67 mg / Carbohydrates: 34 g / Protein: 26 g / Sodium: 1176 mg / Fat: 25 g (Saturated Fat: 11 g) / Potassium: 288 mg.

HOT BROWN

Makes 8 Servings

- 2 tablespoons butter *or* margarine
- ¼ cup all-purpose flour
- 2 cups milk
- ¼ cup shredded sharp cheddar cheese (1 ounce)
- ½ cup grated Parmesan cheese
- ½ teaspoon Worcestershire sauce
- 16 slices toast
- 1 pound cooked turkey, thinly sliced
- 8 slices tomato
- 8 strips bacon, cooked until nearly done

❖ ❖ ❖

Kentucky Hospitality A 200-Year Tradition was a Bicentennial project of the Kentucky Federation of Women's Clubs. The cookbook presents—through essays, illustrations and recipes— a glimpse into the tradition and hospitality of the oldest state west of the Allegheny Mountains.

Mrs. Robert J. Cope, Lexington Woman's Club
Kentucky Hospitality A 200-Year Tradition
Kentucky Federation of Women's Clubs
Louisville
KENTUCKY

1 Preheat the oven to 425°.

2 In a medium saucepan, melt the butter or margarine. Add the flour; stir well. Add the milk, cheddar cheese, *half* of the Parmesan cheese and the Worcestershire sauce all at once. Cook, stirring constantly, until the sauce is thickened and bubbly. Remove from heat; keep warm.

3 Remove the crust from the slices of toast. Cut the toast into triangles. Place the triangles on a baking sheet or in individual baking dishes. Arrange the turkey slices on the toast triangles and pour the hot cheese sauce over all.

4 Place the tomato slices and bacon strips on top of the cheese sauce. Sprinkle with the remaining Parmesan cheese. Bake in the 425° oven for 5 to 10 minutes or until bubbly.

 TIPS FROM OUR KITCHEN

Rather than buy sliced turkey at the deli, you can cook a turkey breast portion and slice it for this recipe.

If you wish, use half turkey and half ham for these sandwiches. Or, substitute ham for all of the turkey.

To make the clean-up easier, line the baking sheet with aluminum foil.

For variety, try making the toast with different types of bread, such as whole wheat, rye and oatmeal. If desired, use toasted English muffins or bagels instead of the toast.

Nutrition Analysis (*Per Serving*): Calories: 299 / Cholesterol: 73 mg / Carbohydrates: 20 g / Protein: 27 g / Sodium: 465 mg / Fat: 12 g (Saturated Fat: 6 g) / Potassium: 409 mg.

HOT BROWN

HAM ALEXANDRIA

HAM ALEXANDRIA

Makes 10 Servings

6	tablespoons butter *or* margarine
8	ounces fresh mushrooms, sliced
2	14-ounce cans artichoke hearts, drained and quartered
3	tablespoons all-purpose flour
2	cups milk
1	cup shredded Swiss cheese
5	English muffins, halved and toasted
10	thin slices cooked ham
2	hard-cooked eggs, chopped
20	pimiento strips (one 2-ounce jar) (optional)

♦ ♦ ♦

Audrey Hammill found a recipe in the 1970s and made a few alterations to create this recipe for Ham Alexandria. Audrey, who loves to entertain casually, recommends serving the dish for brunch.

Audrey G. Hammill
Louisiana Entertains
Rapides Symphony Guild
Alexandria
LOUISIANA

1 In a large skillet, melt *2 tablespoons* of the butter or margarine. Add the mushrooms; cook and stir for 2 to 3 minutes. Add the artichoke hearts and continue to cook and stir for 3 minutes more. Transfer the mixture to a bowl.

2 In the same skillet, melt the remaining butter or margarine. Add the flour and stir until smooth. Add the milk all at once. Cook and stir until thickened and bubbly. Stir in the Swiss cheese and continue cooking until melted. Add the mushroom-artichoke heart mixture. Season with *salt* and *pepper* to taste; heat through.

3 Arrange the English muffin halves on a platter. Top with the ham slices, then cover generously with the sauce. Garnish with the eggs and, if desired, the pimientos.

TIPS FROM OUR KITCHEN

If desired, use 10 ounces of presliced ham which should equal 10 thin slices. Fold the ham diagonally to fit on the muffin halves.

This dish will stay hotter if you "build" it under the broiler. Place the untoasted muffin halves on the rack of a broiler pan or on a baking sheet. Broil 4 to 5 inches from the heat for 1 to 2 minutes or until the muffins are toasted. Top with the ham slices and broil 1 to 2 minutes to heat through. Transfer to a plate and top with the hot cheese sauce. Garnish with the egg and pimiento, if desired.

Before preheating the broiler, use a ruler to check the distance from the heat source to the top of the food being broiled. Don't just measure to the rack.

Nutrition Analysis (*Per Serving*): Calories: 310 / Cholesterol: 91 mg / Carbohydrates: 27 g / Protein: 16 g / Sodium: 826 mg / Fat: 16 g (Saturated Fat: 8 g) / Potassium: 629 mg.

MONTE CRISTO SANDWICHES

Makes 6 Sandwiches
> Margarine *or* butter, melted
> 3 eggs, slightly beaten
> ⅓ cup milk
> 12 slices sandwich bread
> 6 slices Swiss cheese, cut in half
> 6 slices boiled ham
> Powdered sugar (optional)
> Currant jelly (optional)

✦   ✦   ✦

These Monte Cristo Sandwiches are Ann Elliott's adaptation of the popular sandwiches one finds in Midwestern restaurants. Ann's sandwiches are also quite popular. She tells us that a friend's husband always ordered Monte Cristos whenever he had a chance, so Ann gave his wife the recipe. Now he's able to have his favorite sandwich at home, too. Ann has several suggestions for those who are watching their fat intake, including eliminating the margarine or butter by cooking the sandwiches in a non-stick pan, and using skim milk and light cheese.

Ann Elliott
The Art of Cooking in the 80s
Mayfair Lioness Club
Chicago
ILLINOIS

1 Preheat the oven to 425°. Using a pastry brush, generously grease a 15x10x1-inch baking pan with the melted margarine or butter.

2 In a shallow dish, combine the eggs and milk.

3 For each sandwich, cover one slice of bread with a half slice of cheese, a slice of ham, then a second half slice of cheese. Top with a second slice of bread.

4 Dip each sandwich in the egg-milk mixture, taking care to coat each of the bread slices. Place the sandwiches in the prepared baking pan. Bake in the 425° oven for 15 minutes, turning once.

5 Transfer the sandwiches to a warm serving dish. If desired, sprinkle with powered sugar and serve with currant jelly.

 TIPS FROM OUR KITCHEN

Choose a firm-textured white or whole wheat bread. Both slices of the bread should be fairly well soaked in the egg-milk mixture so they remain soft beneath their crisply browned surfaces.

Another method of cooking these sandwiches is to grill them on a griddle or in a greased skillet. This is a higher-calorie option.

A thin slice of turkey can be added to the sandwich or substituted for the ham.

Spread the bread with Dijon-style mustard before adding the meat and cheese for a tangy variation.

Fresh fruit makes a tasty accompaniment to these sandwiches.

Nutrition Analysis (*Per Sandwich*): Calories: 357 / Cholesterol: 142 mg / Carbohydrates: 26 g / Protein: 22 g / Sodium: 736 mg / Fat: 18 g (Saturated Fat: 8 g) / Potassium: 238 mg.

MONTE CRISTO SANDWICHES

Vagabond Pies

Vagabond Pies

Makes 8 Servings

4	carrots, thinly sliced (2 cups)
3	leeks, thinly sliced (1 cup)
1	cup finely chopped rutabaga
8	tiny new potatoes, chopped, *or* 2 cups chopped peeled potatoes
½	cup shredded fontinella *or* fontina cheese (2 ounces)
½	cup shredded mozzarella cheese (2 ounces)
½	cup snipped fresh parsley
2	teaspoons snipped fresh oregano
2	teaspoons snipped fresh marjoram
2	teaspoons snipped fresh thyme
¼	teaspoon salt
⅛	teaspoon pepper
¼	cup butter *or* margarine, melted
¼	cup olive oil
2	cloves garlic, minced
12	sheets phyllo dough (about 6 ounces)
¼	cup fine dry bread crumbs

◆　◆　◆

Dee Gaynor wanted to find a special dish to take to a party. While at the beauty salon, she and her hairdresser, Kathleen Samuels, came up with Vagabond Pies.

Dee Gaynor
<u>Stanford University Medical
Center Auxiliary Cookbook</u>
Stanford University Medical
Center Auxiliary
Stanford
CALIFORNIA

1 Place the carrots, leeks, rutabaga and potatoes in a steamer basket just above, but not touching, *boiling water.* Cover the pan and steam the vegetables for 10 to 12 minutes or just until the vegetables are tender; drain. Transfer the vegetables to a large bowl. Add the fontinella or fontina cheese, mozzarella cheese, parsley, oregano, marjoram, thyme, salt and pepper. Set aside.

2 Preheat the oven to 350°. In a small bowl, stir together the melted butter or margarine, olive oil and garlic.

3 Cut the phyllo dough sheets into 13½- to 14-inch squares; discard any unused portions of phyllo dough. Stack 6 sheets of phyllo, brushing *each* sheet with the butter or margarine mixture and sprinkling every other sheet lightly with the bread crumbs.

4 Cut *each* stack into *4* squares. Place *one-eighth* of the vegetable mixture (about ¾ cup) in the center of *each* square. Fold the sides of the dough toward the center to form a pouch. Pinch well to seal. Place the packets in a shallow baking pan. Brush the outsides with additional butter or margarine mixture. Repeat with the remaining phyllo sheets, butter or margarine mixture and vegetable mixture.

5 Bake in the 350° oven for 30 to 35 minutes or until the pouches are lightly browned. Serve immediately.

Nutrition Analysis (*Per Serving*): Calories: 290 / Cholesterol: 26 mg / Carbohydrates: 31 g / Protein: 8 g / Sodium: 290 mg / Fat: 16 g (Saturated Fat: 5 g) / Potassium: 360 mg.

SPINACH STRATA

Makes 6 Servings
- ½   1-pound loaf French bread *or* other bread, sliced
- 2   tablespoons margarine *or* butter
- 1   cup chopped onion
- 2   10-ounce packages frozen chopped spinach, thawed and well drained
- 1   teaspoon dried dillweed
- ½   teaspoon salt
- Dash pepper
- 1½   cups shredded Swiss cheese (6 ounces)
- 3   beaten eggs
- 2½   cups milk

❖   ❖   ❖

Mary Carpenter's friend, who frequently hunted on Mary's Vermont farm, gave her this recipe for Spinach Strata. Mary said that she liked the recipe because "everything in it was very nutritional." Mary told us that this was an easy dish to make when she was working and that it often tasted better when she cooked it and refrigerated it overnight.

Mary Carpenter
Around the World, Around Our Town: Recipes from San Pedro
Friends of the San Pedro Library
San Pedro
CALIFORNIA

1 Grease a 2-quart rectangular baking dish. Cover the bottom of the dish with *half* of the bread slices, trimming them to fit.

2 In a medium saucepan over medium heat, melt the margarine or butter. Add the onion; cook and stir until tender. Stir in the spinach, dillweed, salt and pepper and cook for 3 minutes more.

3 Spread the spinach mixture over the layer of bread in the baking dish. Sprinkle with *1 cup* of the Swiss cheese. Layer the remaining bread slices over the Swiss cheese layer.

4 In a medium bowl, stir together the beaten eggs and milk. Pour the egg-milk mixture over the layers in the baking dish. Cover and refrigerate at least 1 hour or overnight.

5 Preheat the oven to 375°. Remove the cover from the dish and sprinkle the remaining Swiss cheese over the top of the strata. Cover and bake in the 375° oven for 45 minutes. Uncover and bake about 15 minutes more or until the strata is heated through. Let the strata stand, covered, for 10 minutes before cutting it into squares for serving.

 TIPS FROM OUR KITCHEN

To use fresh spinach in this recipe, carefully wash and trim 2 pounds. Cook the spinach as directed with the onion, adding only a portion of the spinach at a time and stirring the cooked portion to the side as it wilts.

If available, use 1 tablespoon of fresh dill instead of the dried dillweed in this recipe.

Monterey Jack cheese can be substituted for the Swiss cheese in this recipe, or you can use low-fat Swiss cheese instead.

Nutrition Analysis (*Per Serving*): Calories: 371 / Cholesterol: 140 mg / Carbohydrates: 32 g / Protein: 21 g / Sodium: 643 mg / Fat: 18 g (Saturated Fat: 8 g) / Potassium: 493 mg.

SPINACH STRATA

SPINACH QUICHE APPETIZERS

CHICKEN BRUNCH CASSEROLE

SEAFOOD PIE

SEAFOOD PIE

Makes 6 to 8 Servings

2	tablespoons butter *or* margarine
¼	cup chopped green sweet pepper
¼	cup sliced green onion
¼	cup chopped celery
1	4½-ounce jar sliced mushrooms, drained
1	10-ounce package frozen artichoke hearts, thawed
8	ounces lump crabmeat
8	ounces shrimp, cooked and peeled
1	cup shredded cheddar cheese (4 ounces)
¼	cup grated Parmesan cheese
¼	cup mayonnaise
1	tablespoon lemon juice
1	teaspoon Worcestershire sauce
	Several dashes bottled hot pepper sauce
1	egg, beaten
1	8-ounce can sliced water chestnuts, drained (optional)
1	9-inch deep-dish pie shell, partially baked
¼	cup slivered almonds

◆　◆　◆

Mrs. Paul Brock
<u>*One of a Kind*</u>
The Junior League of Mobile,
Incorporated
Mobile
ALABAMA

1 Preheat the oven to 350°.

2 In a large skillet, melt the butter or margarine. Add the green sweet pepper, green onion, celery and mushrooms. Cook and stir until the vegetables are tender, but not brown. Remove from heat.

3 Coarsely chop the artichoke hearts. Add the artichoke hearts, crabmeat, shrimp, *¾ cup* of the cheddar cheese, the Parmesan cheese, mayonnaise, lemon juice, Worcestershire sauce, bottled hot pepper sauce, egg and water chestnuts, if using, to the skillet. Stir well to combine.

4 Transfer the seafood mixture to the partially baked pie shell and bake in the 350° oven for 20 minutes. Sprinkle with the almonds and the remaining *¼ cup* cheddar cheese. Bake for 10 minutes more. Let the pie stand for 5 minutes before cutting it into wedges.

TIPS FROM OUR KITCHEN

To partially bake a pie shell, press a double thickness of foil into a pastry-lined 9-inch pie plate. Bake in a 450° oven for 8 minutes. Remove the foil and bake for 4 to 5 minutes more or until the pie crust is set and dry. (Using the foil prevents the pie shell from puffing up as it bakes.)

If desired, use 1 cup sliced fresh mushrooms instead of the canned mushrooms. You can also substitute canned crab and shrimp if fresh are unavailable.

Nutrition Analysis (*Per Serving*): Calories: 525 / Cholesterol: 269 mg / Carbohydrates: 27 g / Protein: 40g / Sodium: 1,097 mg / Fat: 29 g (Saturated Fat: 11 g) / Potassium: 596 mg.

NOODLE KUGEL

1   8-ounce package noodles
      (about 4 cups)
4   eggs
¾   cup sugar
1 to 2   teaspoons lemon extract
1   teaspoon vanilla
2   8-ounce cartons dairy sour
      cream
2   cups cottage cheese
1   cup milk
2   tablespoons butter *or*
      margarine
1½   teaspoons sugar
½   teaspoon ground cinnamon
2   tablespoons butter *or*
      margarine, cut into small
      pieces

◆   ◆   ◆

Jane Gold tells us that when she married, she was given this recipe for Noodle Kugel by her mother-in-law. Since then, Jane has passed the recipe along to her daughter and daughter-in-law. The Gold family enjoys this dish often, and always with pot roast. We think Noodle Kugel is destined to become a favorite of your family too!

Jane Gold
Tender Loving Care
The Auxiliary to the Broome
County Medical Society
Vestal
NEW YORK

1 Preheat the oven to 350°.

2 Cook the noodles according to the package directions. Drain and set aside.

3 In a large mixing bowl, beat the eggs, ¾ cup sugar, lemon extract and vanilla. Add the sour cream, cottage cheese and milk and mix well. Stir in the cooked and drained noodles.

4 In a 13x9x2-inch baking pan, melt the 2 tablespoons butter or margarine. Add the noodle mixture to the baking pan.

 TIPS FROM OUR KITCHEN

This recipe can be halved and baked in an 8x8x2-inch baking pan if you desire. Bake in the 350° oven about 1 hour or until the kugel tests done.

If you don't have lemon extract, increase the vanilla to 2 teaspoons.

If you're watching the amount of fat in your diet, choose reduced fat sour cream and cottage cheese for this recipe.

5 In a small bowl, stir together the 1½ teaspoons sugar and the cinnamon. Sprinkle the mixture on top of the noodles, then dot with the 2 tablespoons butter or margarine.

6 Bake in the 350° oven for 1 hour to 1 hour and 15 minutes or until a knife inserted near the center comes out clean. The top should be nicely browned. Cool slightly before slicing into squares.

Use the knife test to check for doneness. Insert a knife near the center of the kugel. If it comes out clean, the kugel is done. To avoid having the browned topping "clean" the knife as it is pulled out, enlarge the hole slightly by moving the knife from side to side when you insert it.

Nutrition Analysis *(Per Serving):* Calories: 309 / Cholesterol: 105 mg / Carbohydrates: 31 g / Protein: 11 g / Sodium: 233 mg / Fat: 16 g (Saturated Fat: 9 g) / Potassium: 154 mg.

NOODLE KUGEL

BRUNCH SAUSAGE CASSEROLE

BRUNCH SAUSAGE CASSEROLE

Makes 8 Servings

- 1 pound bulk pork sausage
- 1 cup quick-cooking grits
- 2 tablespoons butter *or* margarine
- 4 eggs, beaten
- 1/3 cup milk
- 1/2 teaspoon salt
- 2 cups shredded sharp cheddar cheese (8 ounces)

♦ ♦ ♦

Gordon Folger, Director of the Women's Center, told us that the center was originally established in 1976 to provide outreach services to women being released from prison. The center now provides services to all women in the Wake County area. Services include peer counseling, personal growth/support groups, information and referral services, and a career development program. Olive Fox, the woman who contributed Brunch Sausage Casserole to the cookbook, was one of the center's devoted volunteers.

Olive Fox
Pot Luck with
The Women's Center
The Women's Center
Raleigh
NORTH CAROLINA

1 Preheat the oven to 350°. Grease a 2-quart square baking dish. Set aside.

2 In large skillet over medium-high heat, cook the sausage until browned, stirring to break up the meat. Drain on paper towels.

3 Cook the grits according to package directions, omitting the salt. Stir in the butter or margarine until melted. Stir in the sausage, eggs, milk, salt and *1¼ cups* of the cheese.

4 Spread the sausage mixture in the prepared baking dish. Bake, uncovered, in the 350° oven for 40 to 45 minutes or until a knife inserted near the center comes out clean.

5 Sprinkle the casserole with the remaining cheese. Bake for 2 to 3 minutes more or until the cheese melts. Let the casserole stand for 10 to 15 minutes before cutting it into squares.

TIPS FROM OUR KITCHEN

Reduced-fat cheddar cheese works well in this recipe. Turkey breakfast sausage is another possible low-fat substitution.

Grits are the ground form of hominy—dried corn with the hull and germ removed. Like popcorn and sweet corn, both the yellow and white varieties are available. Store hominy grits in an airtight container in a cool, dry place up to six months. Hominy, also called samp, was one of the foods Native Americans introduced to the European settlers.

Garnish with finely chopped red pepper and finely snipped parsley to add to the visual appeal of the casserole.

Fresh fruit is a tasty addition to a breakfast or brunch featuring this dish.

Nutrition Analysis (*Per Serving*): Calories: 351 / Cholesterol: 167 mg / Carbohydrates: 17 g / Protein: 17 g / Sodium: 715 mg / Fat: 23 g (Saturated Fat: 11 g) / Potassium: 196 mg.

ONION PIE

Makes 6 Side-Dish Servings

1 cup finely crushed saltine crackers (28)
6 tablespoons margarine *or* butter, melted
2 large onions, thinly sliced (about 2 to 3 cups)
2 eggs, beaten
1 8-ounce carton dairy sour cream
1 tablespoon snipped fresh dill (optional)
½ teaspoon Worcestershire sauce
¼ teaspoon pepper
½ cup shredded cheddar cheese (2 ounces)
4 slices bacon, crisply cooked, drained and crumbled

◆　◆　◆

Evanda Gravitte Moore got this family-favorite recipe for Onion Pie from a study-club friend many years ago. Everyone in her family enjoys the dish—including her boys. Evanda says that she especially likes to serve it at summer barbecues.

Evanda Gravitte Moore
Perennials: A Southern
Celebration of Foods and Flavors
The Junior Service
League of Gainesville
Gainesville
GEORGIA

1 Preheat the oven to 350°. Grease a 9-inch pie plate. Set aside.

2 In a small bowl, stir together the crushed saltines and *4 tablespoons* of the melted margarine or butter. Press into the prepared pie plate. Set aside.

3 In a medium skillet, cook and stir the onions in the remaining margarine or butter for 5 to 10 minutes or until tender. Spread the onions evenly in the cracker crust.

4 In a small bowl, stir together the beaten eggs, sour cream, dill (if using), Worcestershire sauce and pepper. Pour the egg mixture over the onions. Sprinkle with the cheddar cheese and then with the bacon.

5 Bake in the 350° oven for 25 to 30 minutes or until the pie is puffed and just set. Let the pie stand for 5 minutes before serving. Cut into wedges.

TIPS FROM OUR KITCHEN

Use lightly salted or unsalted saltine crackers and reduced-fat sour cream, if desired.

Other cheeses can be substituted for the cheddar cheese, so you may want to experiment with the recipe.

If fresh dill isn't available, substitute 1 teaspoon dried dillweed.

If you have a food processor, you'll save time by using it to crush the crackers and slice the onions.

Many cooks prefer to cook bacon in their microwave ovens. You can find instructions for micro-cooking bacon on the bacon package or in your microwave manual.

The bacon adds color and flavor, but it can be omitted, if you prefer.

Nutrition Analysis (*Per Serving*): Calories: 362 / Cholesterol: 101 mg / Carbohydrates: 19 g / Protein: 8 g / Sodium: 483 mg / Fat: 29 g (Saturated Fat: 10 g) / Potassium: 261 mg.

ONION PIE

SHOWHOUSE SUN-UP RICE

SHOWHOUSE SUN-UP RICE

Makes 6 Servings

8	slices bacon
½	cup chopped onion
½	cup chopped green sweet pepper
4	cups cooked rice
¾	cup water
½	teaspoon salt
¼	teaspoon pepper
1½	cups shredded sharp cheddar cheese (6 ounces)
6	eggs

♦ ♦ ♦

Lynn Higbee does at least 95 percent of his family's cooking. He mainly uses this recipe when entertaining because it's easy to make ahead and it serves a lot of people. In fact, it serves so many people, Lynn was able to make enough for the Everywoman's Resource Center's Designer's Showhouse Mother's Day Brunch (an annual fund-raiser for the organization). Lynn suggests trying curry, fresh red pepper or almonds in the dish for a different taste.

Lynn Higbee
Dinner by Design
Everywoman's Resource Center
Topeka
KANSAS

1 In a 12-inch skillet, cook the bacon until crisp. Transfer the bacon to paper towels to drain; reserve *1 tablespoon* of the bacon drippings.

2 Add the onion and green sweet pepper to the drippings in the skillet. Cook and stir until the vegetables are tender, but not brown. Stir in the cooked rice, water, salt and pepper. Stir in *1 cup* of the cheddar cheese.

3 Using the back of a spoon, make *6* indentations in the top of the rice mixture. Break *1* egg into a custard cup. Carefully pour the egg into *1* of the rice indentations. Repeat with the remaining eggs in each of the remaining

indentations. Sprinkle the remaining cheddar cheese and the bacon over all.

4 Cover the skillet and cook over medium heat for 8 to 10 minutes or until the eggs are set and the cheddar cheese is melted. Serve immediately.

 TIPS FROM OUR KITCHEN

You'll need 1 medium onion or 4 green onions to yield the ½ cup of chopped onion called for in this recipe.

Red or yellow sweet peppers can be substituted for all or part of the green sweet pepper in this recipe.

For 4 cups of cooked rice, you'll need to start with 1⅓ cups of uncooked white or brown rice. Or, you can use a wild rice mixture. If you normally add salt to rice during cooking, you'll probably want to omit the salt called for in this recipe.

For a hotter flavor, substitute hot pepper cheese for the cheddar cheese in this recipe and serve salsa on the side.

Nutrition Analysis (*Per Serving*): Calories: 401 / Cholesterol: 252 mg / Carbohydrates: 32 g / Protein: 19 g / Sodium: 553 mg / Fat: 21 g (Saturated Fat: 10 g) / Potassium: 197 mg.

chapter four

vegetables
& fruits

The main course of any meal can only be enhanced when served with one of these dazzling side dishes. Roasted or grilled meats are shown off to perfection when accompanied by Onions au Gratin or Rosemary Potatoes; sandwiches are transformed into noteworthy partners when paired with Golden Stuffed Potatoes or Fresh Pineapple and Strawberries in Shells; or a strata or casserole is turned into a star attraction by a side show of Peas with Mint and Orange Peel or a crunchy Three-Lettuce Salad. From stand-alone Spaghetti Squash Tomato Toss to a fabulous finale of Fruit Pizza, this chapter is full of inspirational culinary surprises.

ONIONS AU GRATIN

ONIONS AU GRATIN

Makes 6 Servings
- 2 tablespoons butter *or* margarine
- 5 medium onions, thinly sliced and separated into rings (5 cups)
- 2 cups shredded cheddar cheese (8 ounces)
- ⅓ cup packaged biscuit mix
- ⅛ teaspoon pepper
- ½ cup shredded cheddar cheese (2 ounces) (optional)

When recipes for the Junior League of Rockford's cookbook were requested from league members and popular local restaurants, between 3,000 and 5,000 recipes were submitted. Each member taste-tested ten recipes, and then completed an evaluation for each one. The most popular recipes were then tested a second time. The result was a wonderful collection of super recipes such as this one for Onions au Gratin.

Brunch Basket
The Junior League of Rockford
Rockford
ILLINOIS

1 Preheat the oven to 350°. Grease a 1½-quart casserole dish; set aside.

2 In a large saucepan, melt the butter or margarine. Add the onions and cook, covered, over medium-low heat for 10 to 15 minutes or until tender, stirring occasionally. Remove from heat.

3 Stir the 2 cups cheddar cheese, the biscuit mix and pepper into the onion mixture. Transfer the mixture to the prepared casserole dish. Sprinkle with the ½ cup cheddar cheese, if desired. Bake the casserole, uncovered, in the 350° oven for 30 minutes. Serve immediately.

TIPS FROM OUR KITCHEN

The dry bulb onions that are available in most stores between April and August are generally milder, sweeter and less pungent than the so-called fall/winter onions. Dry bulb onions have thin, light outer skins and a high water and sugar content. They are fragile and bruise easily; they can be stored in the refrigerator for several weeks. The fall/winter, or storage, onions have a thicker, darker outer skin, a lower water content and a more pungent flavor. When they are stored in a cool, dry, well-ventilated spot, they will keep for several months.

If you want to cut the fat in this recipe, use only half as much butter or margarine to cook the onions. Add about ¼ cup *water* instead.

Use a fork or onion-holder to steady the onion when cutting it into slices. Transfer the slices to a large bowl or pan and use your fingers or a fork to separate them into rings. Or, if you don't mind half slices, use your food processor to slice the onions.

Nutrition Analysis (*Per Serving*): Calories: 255 / Cholesterol: 50 mg / Carbohydrates: 14 g / Protein: 11 g / Sodium: 353 mg / Fat: 17 g (Saturated Fat: 10 g) / Potassium: 199 mg.

ROSEMARY POTATOES

Makes 3 to 4 Servings

1	large clove garlic, minced
1½	teaspoons snipped fresh rosemary
2	tablespoons olive oil
1½	pounds baking potatoes, peeled and cubed
½	teaspoon salt
⅛	teaspoon freshly ground pepper
2 to 3	sprigs fresh rosemary (optional)

❖ ❖ ❖

What's Cooking? was put together by a longtime volunteer for Hospice Care of D.C. Founded in 1977, Hospice Care of D.C. is the oldest non-profit, volunteer-assisted hospice providing services primarily in home-based settings to District residents. Proceeds from cookbook sales help the organization to continue offering their compassionate and essential services.

What's Cooking?
Hospice Care of the
District of Columbia
Washington
D.C.

1 In a large skillet, cook and stir the garlic and rosemary in the olive oil for 1 to 2 minutes over medium heat. Add the potatoes, salt and pepper.

2 Cook for 5 minutes, stirring occasionally. Reduce the heat to medium-low and cook about 20 minutes more, turning often, until the potatoes are brown and crisp. Garnish with the rosemary sprigs, if desired.

 TIPS FROM OUR KITCHEN

To snip fresh rosemary, remove the leaves, place in a deep container such as a 1-cup measure and finely snip them using kitchen scissors. Or, you can use a knife on a cutting board to chop them.

If you don't have fresh rosemary on hand, try substituting fresh basil, savory or thyme.

When new potatoes are in season, substitute them for the baking potatoes. No need to peel new potatoes, just cut them into quarters and they're ready for cooking.

If you need fresh herbs, and don't grow your own, look for them at your local farmers' market. They usually have a wonderful selection of fresh herbs at reasonable prices.

Nutrition Analysis (*Per Serving*): Calories: 244 / Cholesterol: 0 mg / Carbohydrates: 38 g / Protein: 3 g / Sodium: 365 mg / Fat: 9 g (Saturated Fat: 1 g) / Potassium: 624 mg.

ROSEMARY POTATOES

GOLDEN STUFFED POTATOES

116

GOLDEN STUFFED POTATOES

Makes 12 Servings
- 6 large baking potatoes
- 1 cup shredded cheddar cheese (4 ounces)
- 2 tablespoons butter *or* margarine
- 1 8-ounce carton dairy sour cream
- 1/3 cup chopped green onion
- 2 tablespoons butter *or* margarine (optional)

♦ ♦ ♦

Recipes in <u>Tidewater on the Half Shell</u> were chosen with great care by the Junior League of Nor-folk—Virginia Beach, Inc. They established a committee that tested each recipe three times. Apparently, the time they took compiling their cookbook was well spent—now it is in its fifth printing and last year it raised $20,000 for the league's community projects. Projects that benefited from the sales include Growing Up Great (prenatal care), Pals Library (literacy) and Career Clothes Closet (inexpensive clothing sales).

<u>*Tidewater on the Half Shell*</u>
The Junior League of Norfolk—
Virginia Beach, Inc.
Norfolk
VIRGINIA

1 Preheat the oven to 400°.

2 Thoroughly scrub the baking pota-toes with a brush. Pat the potatoes dry and prick with a fork. Bake in the 400° oven about 1 hour or until tender.

3 Meanwhile, in a medium saucepan over low heat, stir together the cheese and the 2 tablespoons butter or margarine; heat and stir until the cheese is melted.

4 Remove the butter-cheese mixture from the heat; stir in the sour cream, green onion, 1/4 teaspoon *salt* and 1/4 teaspoon *pepper*.

5 Reduce the oven temperature to 350°. Cut the potatoes in *half* length-wise. Using a spoon, gently scoop out the pulp, leaving a thin shell.

6 Using an electric mixer on low speed or a potato masher, beat or mash the pulp. Add the sour cream mixture; mix well.

7 Spoon the sour cream-potato mixture into the potato skins. Place the skins in a 3-quart rectangular baking dish. Dot with the 2 tablespoons butter or mar-garine, if desired. Bake, uncovered, in the 350° oven about 15 minutes or until heated through.

 TIPS FROM OUR KITCHEN

Choose fresh potatoes of similar size and shape with clean, smooth skins and a firm texture. Avoid those with green spots, soft or moldy areas or wilted skins. Russets are a good choice for this recipe because they have thick skins. Long white varieties with thin skins and some yellow varieties are also suitable for baking.

Since 1 large potato weighs about 7 ounces, 6 large potatoes will weigh slightly more than 2 1/2 pounds.

If desired, use reduced-fat cheddar cheese and sour cream.

Sometimes called twice-baked potatoes, these are a great make-ahead choice. Securely wrap the stuffed halves in heavy-duty aluminum foil and freeze them up to 2 months. To reheat frozen potatoes, unwrap and place them on a baking sheet. Bake in a 375° oven for 45 minutes.

Nutrition Analysis (*Per Serving*): Calories: 186 / Cholesterol: 23 mg / Carbohydrates: 22 g / Protein: 5 g / Sodium: 141 mg / Fat: 9 g (Saturated Fat: 6 g) / Potassium: 348 mg.

SOUFFLÉ POTATOES

Makes 8 Servings

- 3 cups mashed potatoes (5 or 6 potatoes)
- 1 cup cream-style cottage cheese
- ½ cup dairy sour cream
- 3 egg yolks, well beaten
- 3 tablespoons chopped onion
- 3 tablespoons chopped pimiento (optional)
- 2 tablespoons butter *or* margarine, melted
- 1 clove garlic, minced
- ½ teaspoon salt
- Dash pepper
- 3 egg whites, stiffly beaten
- 1 tablespoon butter *or* margarine

◆ ◆ ◆

Phyllis Hallene tasted her sister-in-law's recipe for Soufflé Potatoes about twenty years ago and immediately requested the recipe. Phyllis suggests if you're a garlic lover, like she is, that you add a little extra to the dish. Although Soufflé Potatoes deflate slightly if not served immediately, Phyllis assures us that they'll still be absolutely delicious.

Phyllis Hallene
Return Engagement
The Junior Board of the Quad City Symphony Orchestra Association
Davenport
IOWA

1 Preheat the oven to 350°. Grease a 2-quart casserole; set aside.

2 In a large mixing bowl, stir together the mashed potatoes, cottage cheese, sour cream, egg yolks, onion, pimiento (if using), the 2 tablespoons melted butter or margarine, garlic, salt and pepper.

3 Beat with an electric mixer on medium speed until the mixture is light and fluffy, scraping the sides of the bowl. Gently fold in the beaten egg whites.

4 Carefully spoon the mixture into the prepared casserole. Dot with the 1 tablespoon butter or margarine.

5 Bake in the 350° oven about 1 hour or until the casserole is puffed and the top is golden. Serve immediately.

TIPS FROM OUR KITCHEN

For 3 cups mashed potatoes, peel and cut up 2 pounds potatoes. Keep the peeled and cut pieces immersed in cold water to prevent them from darkening. Cook, covered, in a small amount of boiling water for 20 to 25 minutes or until the potato pieces are tender, adding more water if necessary. Mash with a potato masher, slotted spoon or electric mixer.

If you want this to be a make-ahead dish, prepare the potatoes as directed up until the point of baking. Then, refrigerate the prepared potato mixture, covered, up to 4 hours. Uncover and bake about 1 hour or until the potatoes are puffed and the top is golden.

For a tangier flavor, use flavored sour cream dip such as garlic, chive or French onion in place of the sour cream in the recipe.

Nutrition Analysis (*Per Serving*): Calories: 224 / Cholesterol: 102 mg / Carbohydrates: 25 g / Protein: 8 g / Sodium: 331 mg / Fat: 11 g (Saturated Fat: 6 g) / Potassium: 478 mg.

SOUFFLÉ POTATOES

PARTY GREEN BEANS

PARTY GREEN BEANS

Makes 8 Servings

Green Beans:

- 2   10-ounce packages frozen French-style green beans
- 1   cup canned bean sprouts, drained
- 1   8-ounce can sliced water chestnuts, drained
- ¼   cup grated Parmesan cheese and ¼ cup shredded Swiss cheese, mixed

Cream Sauce:

- 3   tablespoons butter *or* margarine
- 2   tablespoons flour
- ¼   teaspoon salt
- ⅛   teaspoon pepper
- Dash of ground red pepper
- 1½   cups light cream *or* half-and-half
- ½   teaspoon Worcestershire sauce
- ½   cup chopped almonds

◆   ◆   ◆

Recipes for interesting, quick and delicious vegetables are every good cook's mainstay. Here is one of Brenda Chattaway's favorites that she likes to serve with ham or pork roast.

Brenda Chattaway
<u>The Texas Experience</u>
The Richardson Woman's Club, Inc.
Richardson
TEXAS

1   Preheat oven to 375°. Grease a shallow 1½- or 2-quart rectangular baking dish.

2   To make the green beans: In a medium saucepan, cook the green beans in boiling water for 5 minutes. Drain.

3   In the prepared baking dish, layer the green beans, bean sprouts, water chestnuts and mixed cheeses.

4   To prepare the cream sauce: In a medium saucepan, melt *2 tablespoons* of the butter or margarine. Stir in the flour, salt, pepper and red pepper. Add the light cream and Worcestershire sauce. Cook and stir until thickened and bubbly.

5   Pour the sauce over the vegetable mixture, lifting the mixture gently with a fork so the sauce will penetrate. Do not stir.

6   Bake, uncovered, in the 375° oven for 20 to 30 minutes or until bubbly and heated through.

7   Melt the remaining butter in a small saucepan; add the almonds. Stir to coat well. Sprinkle the almonds over the casserole and serve.

 TIPS FROM OUR KITCHEN

If you like your Party Green Beans a little creamier, use only 4 teaspoons of flour.

If you'd like more of a toastier nut flavor from the almonds, omit tossing them in butter and toast them in the oven. To toast nuts in the oven, spread them into a thin layer in a shallow baking pan. Bake in a 350° oven for 5 to 10 minutes or until the nuts are light golden brown, stirring once or twice.

Nutrition Analysis (*Per Serving*): Calories: 208 / Cholesterol: 34 mg / Carbohydrates: 12 g / Protein: 7 g / Sodium: 277 mg / Fat: 16 g (Saturated Fat: 8 g) / Potassium: 235 mg.

SPAGHETTI SQUASH TOMATO TOSS

Makes 8 Servings
- 1 3½-pound spaghetti squash
- 1 medium onion, coarsely chopped
- 1 tablespoon olive oil
- 5 medium tomatoes, peeled, seeded and coarsely chopped
- ½ cup snipped fresh basil
- ¼ cup snipped parsley
- 2 cloves garlic minced
- ¾ teaspoon salt
- ¼ teaspoon pepper
- 3 medium zucchini, sliced in ¼-inch pieces
- Parmesan cheese *or* parsley sprigs

❖ ❖ ❖

According to Carol Shepard, one of the editors of Heavenly Hosts, *Spaghetti Squash Tomato Toss is "a great alternative to spaghetti" and appeals to everyone, even those who aren't "true vegetable lovers." Carol adapted this recipe to suit her family's liking—especially her children's—and says the dish is an excellent way to use up surplus zucchini and tomatoes.*

Heavenly Hosts Committee
Heavenly Hosts
Presbyterian Women of The Bryn Mawr Presbyterian Church
Bryn Mawr
PENNSYLVANIA

1 Preheat the oven to 350°.

2 Using the tip of a sharp knife or the tines of a fork, pierce the squash in several places. Place in a 13x9x2-inch baking pan. Bake in the 350° oven for 1 hour and 15 minutes.

3 Meanwhile, in a large skillet, cook the onion in the olive oil until tender. Add the tomatoes, basil, parsley, garlic, salt and pepper. Bring to a boil. Add the zucchini and cook, covered, for 3 minutes. Uncover and cook for 8 to 10 minutes more or until the zucchini is crisp-tender. Keep warm.

4 Carefully slice the squash in half. Remove the seeds and discard. Use a fork to shred the squash into long strands into a bowl. Pour the sauce over the spaghetti squash; toss. Garnish with Parmesan cheese or parsley sprigs. Serve immediately.

 TIPS FROM OUR KITCHEN

Spaghetti squash is a bright yellow, football-shaped vegetable with pale yellow, stringy flesh that resembles spaghetti when cooked. It has a mildly sweet flavor.

It's easier to "shred" the spaghetti squash if you use a hot pad to hold the halved squash at an angle. Use a fork to rake the stringy pulp from the shell into the bowl.

Store olive oil at room temperature up to 6 months, or in the refrigerator up to 1 year. When olive oil is chilled, it gets too thick to pour, so let it stand at room temperature for a few minutes or run warm water over the bottle before using.

Nutrition Analysis (*Per Serving*): Calories: 95 / Cholesterol: 1 mg / Carbohydrates: 16 g / Protein: 3 g / Sodium: 262 mg / Fat: 3 g (Saturated Fat: 1 g) / Potassium: 463 mg.

SPAGHETTI SQUASH TOMATO TOSS

FRESH ASPARAGUS WITH ORANGE HOLLANDAISE SAUCE

FRESH ASPARAGUS WITH ORANGE HOLLANDAISE SAUCE

Makes 4 Servings

- 1 pound fresh asparagus spears
- 2 egg yolks
- 1 teaspoon grated orange peel
- 2 tablespoons orange juice
- Dash salt
- Dash pepper
- ¼ cup butter *or* margarine, cut into tablespoons
- ¼ cup dairy sour cream
- Finely shredded orange peel (optional)

◆   ◆   ◆

It's hard to improve the taste of perfectly prepared fresh asparagus, but Terri Brusco of Longview, Washington, gives us an inspired way to enjoy the tasty green spears. This orange-flavored variation of a traditional Hollandaise sauce served over asparagus is an unexpected treat for Terri's lucky dinner party guests.

Terri Brusco
Cabaret Cuisine
Longview Junior Service League
Longview
WASHINGTON

1 Snap off and discard woody bases from the fresh asparagus. If desired, scrape off scales. Cook, covered, in a small amount of boiling water for 8 to 10 minutes or until crisp-tender. Drain and set aside, keeping hot.

2 In a small saucepan using a wire whisk, combine the egg yolks, grated orange peel, orange juice, salt and pepper.

3 Over low heat, continue whisking, adding the butter, *one tablespoon* at a time, until the butter is melted and the sauce is thickened (about 7 minutes).

4 Remove the saucepan from the heat and stir in the sour cream. Return the sauce to the stovetop and heat through but *do not* boil.

5 Transfer the hot asparagus to a warm serving dish. Pour the sauce over the asparagus. Garnish with the finely shredded orange peel, if desired.

 TIPS FROM OUR KITCHEN

If you know you're going to be short on time, make this sauce ahead and store it, covered, in the refrigerator. Then, before serving, reheat the sauce over low heat just until warm.

Try this sauce over your favorite fish fillets or fish steaks too.

Nutrition Analysis *(Per Serving)*: Calories: 185 / Cholesterol: 144 mg / Carbohydrates: 5 g / Protein: 4 g / Sodium: 164 mg / Fat: 17 g (Saturated Fat: 10 g) / Potassium: 292 mg.

PEAS WITH MINT AND ORANGE PEEL

Makes 6 Servings

2	pounds fresh peas (3 cups shelled)
½	cup water
⅛	teaspoon salt
¼	cup butter *or* margarine, cut up
3 to 4	teaspoons finely shredded orange peel
2	tablespoons snipped fresh mint *or* ½ teaspoon dried mint, crushed

Dash salt
Dash pepper

◆　　◆　　◆

When we spoke with Terry Robinette's daughter, Mary Beth Windsich, she told us about her fond memories of the Robinette's traditional Sunday dinners. Mary Beth said that her mother "always made something nice." Peas with Mint and Orange Peel was one of Terry's special dishes. Mary Beth told us that she believes the recipe came from a relative in Kentucky on her father's side of the family.

Terry Robinette
Madonna Heights Ladies
Auxiliary Favorite Recipe
Collections
Madonna Heights Ladies
Auxiliary
Huntington
NEW YORK

1 Shell the peas and rinse in cold water.

2 In a medium saucepan, bring the water and salt to a boil. Add the peas and return to a boil. Reduce heat. Cover and simmer for 10 to 12 minutes or until the peas are crisp-tender.

3 Drain the cooked peas. Add the butter or margarine, orange peel and mint; toss to coat. Season to taste with the salt and pepper. Serve immediately.

 TIPS FROM OUR KITCHEN

When shopping for fresh peas, look for small, plump, bright green, shiny pods that are filled with medium-size peas. Refrigerate unshelled and unwashed peas in a plastic bag up to 2 days.

To micro-cook fresh peas: Place them in a microwave-safe casserole with 2 tablespoons *water*. Micro-cook, covered, on 100% power (high) for 4 to 6 minutes or until the peas are crisp-tender, stirring once.

If fresh peas aren't available, substitute one 16-ounce package frozen peas and cook according to the package directions.

Spearmint and peppermint are the two most widely used mints. Peppermint has a sharp, pungent flavor, while spearmint has a more delicate flavor.

Instead of trying to chop fresh mint with a knife, place the leaves in a glass measuring cup and snip with scissors.

If you are using dried mint, measure it, then crush it between your fingers to release the aromatic oils.

To shred orange peel: Push a clean orange across a fine shredding surface to make very fine strips.

Nutrition Analysis (*Per Serving*): Calories: 131 / Cholesterol: 21 mg / Carbohydrates: 12 g / Protein: 4 g / Sodium: 214 mg / Fat: 8 g (Saturated Fat: 5 g) / Potassium: 141 mg.

PEAS WITH MINT AND ORANGE PEEL

TABOULI

TABOULI

Makes 6 Servings

1	cup bulgur
1	small cucumber, seeded and chopped (1 cup)
1	tomato, chopped (⅔ cup)
1	small sweet green pepper, seeded and chopped (½ cup)
¼	cup sliced green onion
½	cup snipped parsley
½	cup olive oil
⅓	cup lemon juice
3	tablespoons water
2	tablespoons snipped fresh mint *or* 1 teaspoon dried mint, crushed
⅛	teaspoon salt
⅛	teaspoon pepper
	Leaf lettuce

◆   ◆   ◆

Beth Yohe's recipe for Tabouli came from several different recipes that she combined to create one to "suit her own tastes." Beth employed this recipe when she taught a food preparation course at the local Jewish Community Center. She suggests serving the salad on a bed of curly lettuce to enhance the presentation of the dish.

Beth Yohe

Best of Friends

Friends of the Maitland

Public Library

Maitland

FLORIDA

1 In a large bowl, combine the bulgur, cucumber, tomato, sweet green pepper and green onion. Set aside.

2 In a small bowl, stir together the parsley, olive oil, lemon juice, water, mint, salt and pepper.

3 Add the parsley mixture to the bulgur mixture and toss to mix. Cover and refrigerate for 4 to 24 hours. Serve the tabouli on a bed of leaf lettuce.

 TIPS FROM OUR KITCHEN

Bulgur (or bulghur) is a parched, cracked wheat product made by soaking, cooking and then drying whole wheat kernels. Five percent of the bran is then removed from the dried, hard wheat kernels, and the remaining kernels are cracked into small pieces. Bulgur is dark tan in color and has a nutty flavor. Store bulgur in an airtight container in a cool, dry place up to 6 months, or indefinitely in the freezer.

Be sure not to purchase cracked wheat breakfast cereal in place of bulgur.

Tabouli (or tabbouleh) is a Middle Eastern dish that can be served on pieces of pita, as an eat-with-a-fork salad or as a dip with celery or sweet green pepper wedges.

Use fresh lemon juice in this recipe, if possible. You'll need 2 medium lemons for ⅓ cup fresh lemon juice. Look for well-shaped fruits with smooth, evenly yellow skin. To get the most juice, choose fruits that are heavy for their size. Leave the lemons at room temperature for about 30 minutes, then roll gently under the palm of your hand. Or, cut the lemons in half and heat in microwave oven on 100% power (high) for 30 to 45 seconds before juicing.

An easy way to snip the parsley and mint is to place the fresh herbs in a deep container, such as a 1-cup glass measure, then snip with kitchen shears.

Nutrition Analysis: (*Per Serving*): Calories: 260 / Cholesterol: 0 mg / Carbohydrates: 23 g / Protein: 4 g / Sodium: 55 mg / Fat: 19 g (Saturated Fat: 3 g) / Potassium: 321 mg.

THREE-LETTUCE SALAD

Makes 6 Servings

2	tablespoons olive oil *or* salad oil
2	tablespoons red wine vinegar
1 to 4	cloves garlic, minced
⅛	teaspoon salt
2	cups torn romaine lettuce
2	cups torn leaf lettuce
2	cups torn butter lettuce
1	11-ounce can mandarin oranges, drained
1	cup seedless red grapes, halved

Red onion, thinly sliced and rings separated

⅓ cup toasted slivered almonds

◆ ◆ ◆

When we spoke with Lorna Reay, she told us that she loves to experiment in the kitchen. Whenever she finds a new recipe, she makes little changes here and there to create her own dish. Such is the case with this recipe for Three-Lettuce Salad. When Lorna served this salad to her in-laws, they raved about it, and still do every time they see her.

The Reay Family
Johnston Schools
Cooking Up A Storm
Johnston PTO
Johnston
IOWA

1 In a screwtop jar, combine the olive oil or salad oil, vinegar, garlic and salt. Cover and shake until well blended. Chill until serving time.

2 In a large salad bowl, combine the romaine, leaf and butter lettuce. Add the mandarin oranges, grapes and as much red onion as you like.

3 To serve: Pour the dressing on top of the salad; toss to coat. Sprinkle with the almonds.

 TIPS FROM OUR KITCHEN

When you're in a hurry, substitute your favorite bottled Italian salad dressing for the homemade dressing used here.

There are several ways to mince garlic: You can use a knife to cut it into tiny pieces, use a garlic press or crush the peeled garlic with the side of a French knife.

You can add some meat, poultry or fish to this recipe to make it a main dish. Smoked turkey would be especially delicious.

Try another oil in place of the olive oil for a subtle change of flavor. Consider using almond oil or walnut oil, and sprinkling the corresponding nuts on top.

For a change of pace, substitute toasted walnuts, pecans, pine nuts or cashews for the almonds.

Nutrition Analysis *(Per Serving)*: Calories: 126 / Cholesterol: 0 mg / Carbohydrates: 13 g / Protein: 3 g / Sodium: 51 mg / Fat: 8 g (Saturated Fat: 1 g) / Potassium: 329 mg.

THREE-LETTUCE SALAD

FRUIT PIZZA

FRUIT PIZZA

Makes 2 Pizzas (24 Servings)

Sugar Cookie Crust:

1	cup butter *or* margarine, softened
1	cup sifted powdered sugar
1/3	cup granulated sugar
1	egg
1/2	teaspoon vanilla
1/4	teaspoon almond extract
2 1/2	cups all-purpose flour
2	teaspoons baking soda
2	teaspoons cream of tartar

Orange Sauce:

1/2	cup granulated sugar
1/4	teaspoon finely shredded orange peel
1/4	teaspoon finely shredded lemon peel
1	cup orange juice
2	tablespoons lemon juice
4	teaspoons cornstarch

Filling:

2	8-ounce packages cream cheese, softened
1	cup sifted powdered sugar
1	teaspoon vanilla
	Fresh fruits of choice (about 7 cups total): sliced peaches, nectarines, strawberries, kiwi fruit, bananas, grapes, apples, mandarin oranges *and/or* raspberries

❖   ❖   ❖

Who says that too many cooks spoil the broth? This delicious dessert is the victorious outcome of a recipe-by-committee!

A Pinch of Salt Lake

The Junior League of Salt Lake City, Inc.

Salt Lake City

UTAH

1 Preheat oven to 325°. Lightly grease two 12-inch pizza pans.

2 To prepare the crust: In a large mixing bowl, cream the butter or margarine, powdered sugar and granulated sugar until light. Add the egg, vanilla and almond extract, beating well.

3 Combine the dry ingredients and add to the creamed mixture, blending thoroughly.

4 Divide the dough in half. With lightly floured hands, pat the dough into the prepared pans. Bake in the 325° oven for 12 to 15 minutes or until golden; cool.

5 To prepare the orange sauce: Combine the sugar, orange and lemon peel, orange and lemon juice and cornstarch in a small saucepan. Cook and stir over medium heat until the mixture is thick. Cook and stir for 2 minutes more. Cover and cool the sauce without stirring.

6 Meanwhile, to prepare the filling: In a medium mixing bowl, beat the cream cheese, powdered sugar and vanilla with an electric mixer until fluffy.

7 Spread the cream cheese mixture over the cooled crusts. Decorate with fruit.

8 Glaze the fruit with the cooled sauce. Chill the pizzas until ready to serve.

TIPS FROM OUR KITCHEN

When you only need one pizza, wrap and seal the extra crust in moisture-vapor-proof wrap and freeze the extra crust for another time; then make only half the filling and orange sauce.

The clusters of tiny grapes on top of the pizza in the photograph are known as champagne grapes. Look for them near the other grapes in the produce section of the grocery store.

Nutrition Analysis *(Per Serving)*: Calories: 267 / Cholesterol: 50 mg / Carbohydrates: 32 g / Protein: 3 g / Sodium: 207 mg / Fat: 15 g (Saturated Fat: 9 g) / Potassium: 168 mg.

24-HOUR SALAD

Makes 16 Servings

- 2 eggs, beaten
- 2 tablespoons sugar
- 2 tablespoons orange juice
- 2 tablespoons vinegar
- 1 tablespoon butter *or* margarine
- Dash salt
- 2 8-ounce cartons dairy sour cream
- 1 cup seedless grapes, halved
- 1 cup dried bananas
- 1 15¼-ounce can pineapple tidbits, drained
- 1 cup pitted bing cherries
- 1 cup finely chopped orange
- 1 cup cantaloupe balls
- 2 plums, sliced
- 2 cups miniature marshmallows
- Lettuce leaves

♦ ♦ ♦

Betty Kracht said that she brings 24-Hour Salad to all of the Little Egypt Council's potluck dinners. She first tasted the salad at a potluck dinner hosted by a different organization when Ethel Porter, a fellow member, presented the unique treat.

Betty Kracht
<u>*Favorite Recipes of*</u>
<u>*Little Egypt Council*</u>
The Little Egypt Council
Telephone Pioneers of America
Centralia
ILLINOIS

1 In a small saucepan, stir together the beaten eggs, sugar, orange juice and vinegar. Cook and stir over medium heat just until thickened. Immediately remove from heat and stir in the butter or margarine and salt. Cool.

2 Place the sour cream into a medium bowl. Gently fold the cooled egg mixture into the sour cream. Cover and refrigerate the dressing while you prepare the fruits.

3 In a large bowl, stir together the grapes, dried bananas, pineapple, cherries, orange, cantaloupe balls, plums and marshmallows.

4 Pour the chilled dressing over the fruit mixture; stir to coat. Cover and refrigerate the salad overnight.

5 To serve, spoon the salad onto lettuce-lined plates.

 TIPS FROM OUR KITCHEN

When you are cooking the dressing, watch carefully. When the mixture starts to thicken, immediately remove the pan from heat. If the dressing cooks too long, the egg will curdle.

You can substitute reduced-fat sour cream or vanilla yogurt for the sour cream, and pineapple juice for the orange juice.

If desired, omit the dried bananas. Just before serving, slice two medium bananas and add them to the salad.

Many kinds of plums are available—mainly from June through September. You may want to try one of the following in this salad recipe: Ace, Casselman, Friar or Queen Ann. Let the plums ripen at room temperature, then refrigerate them up to five days.

Nutrition Analysis (*Per Serving*): Calories: 160 / Cholesterol: 41 mg / Carbohydrates: 20 g / Protein: 3 g / Sodium: 43 mg / Fat: 9 g (Saturated Fat: 5 g) / Potassium: 220 mg.

24-Hour Salad

STRAWBERRY SURPRISE

Makes 12 Servings

- ¾ cup margarine *or* butter, softened
- 3 tablespoons brown sugar
- 2½ cups crushed pretzels
- 1 6-ounce package strawberry-flavored gelatin
- 2 cups boiling water
- 3 10-ounce packages frozen strawberries, thawed and undrained
- 1 8-ounce package cream cheese, softened
- 1 3-ounce package cream cheese, softened
- 1 cup granulated sugar
- 1 cup whipping cream, whipped

Strawberry fans (optional)

◆　　◆　　◆

Lynda remembers that her mother gave her this recipe about nine years ago. Because Lynda works full-time she needs no-fail, simple recipes like this one. She says, "Strawberry Surprise is tempting and delicious—the crust is unique and the color is bright." Lynda also told us that this dish was definitely a compliment-getter.

Lynda Hunter
Deep In The Heart: A Collection of Recipes Dallas Junior Forum
Dallas Junior Forum
Dallas
TEXAS

1 Preheat the oven to 350°

2 In a medium mixing bowl using an electric mixer, cream together the softened margarine or butter and brown sugar until smooth. Stir in the crushed pretzels. Pat the pretzel mixture over the bottom of a 3-quart rectangular baking dish. Bake the pretzel crust in the 350° oven for 10 minutes. Remove from oven; transfer to a wire rack to cool.

3 Meanwhile, dissolve the strawberry-flavored gelatin in the boiling water. Stir in the strawberries. Chill the strawberry mixture in the refrigerator until it is slightly thickened.

4 In a large mixing bowl using the electric mixer, beat together the 8-ounce and 3-ounce packages softened cream cheese and granulated sugar until smooth. Fold the whipped cream into the cream cheese mixture.

5 Evenly spread the cream cheese mixture over the cooled pretzel crust. Spoon the strawberry mixture over the cream cheese layer. Cover and chill for 6 to 24 hours or until firm. To serve, cut into squares and garnish each serving with a strawberry fan, if desired.

 TIPS FROM OUR KITCHEN

You'll need approximately 48 large pretzel twists (6 ounces) to yield the 2½ cups of crushed pretzels called for in this recipe. If desired, substitute unsalted pretzels for all or part of the amount. To crush the pretzels, place them in a heavy plastic bag and flatten them with a rolling pin.

Soften the margarine or butter by placing the unwrapped stick in a mixing bowl and leaving it at room temperature. Or, place the unwrapped margarine stick in a microwave-safe container and micro-cook, uncovered, on 100% power (high) for 15 seconds. *Do not* melt the margarine.

Be sure to thaw the strawberries *before* beginning this recipe or the icy berries will cause the gelatin to set up too fast.

If desired, substitute frozen raspberries and raspberry-flavored gelatin for the strawberries and the strawberry-flavored gelatin in this salad.

Garnish each serving of this salad with additional whipped cream, if desired.

Nutrition Analysis (*Per Serving*): Calories: 506 / Cholesterol: 60 mg / Carbohydrates: 62 g / Protein: 6 g / Sodium: 451 mg / Fat: 29 g (Saturated Fat: 12 g) / Potassium: 148 mg.

FRESH PINEAPPLE AND STRAWBERRIES IN SHELLS

Makes 8 Servings

2 small pineapples
½ cup light rum
¼ cup powdered sugar
3 cups fresh strawberries, washed, hulled and drained
1 cup halved seedless green grapes

◆   ◆   ◆

Jeanne Carpenter, president of the Bonhomme Township Federated Republican Women's Club, tells us, "Our club is very proud to have produced this cookbook to aid in the wonderful work that the Judevine Center for Autism is doing to make life better for autistic individuals and their families." Since its founding in 1970, Judevine has been a pioneer in the treatment, training and research of autism. One hundred percent of the profits from the sale of International Cookbook goes directly to support these efforts.

Mary Lou Bass
International Cookbook
Bonhomme Township Federated Republican Women's Club
Kirkwood
MISSOURI

1 Cut each pineapple lengthwise into quarters. Snip off the brown leaf tips, if desired. Cut the pineapple from the shells in single pieces so that you have 8 long pieces. Place the shells on a tray; cover and refrigerate.

2 Cut the core from the pineapple pieces, discard the core and cut the pineapple pieces into chunks. (You should have about 5 cups.)

3 Place the pineapple chunks in a large bowl. Add the rum and powdered sugar and mix gently. Cover and refrigerate for 24 hours.

4 Slice all but 8 of the strawberries; cover and refrigerate until ready to serve. Halve the grapes, cover and refrigerate until ready to serve.

5 Just before serving, in a large bowl, combine the sliced strawberries, halved grapes and the pineapple chunks; toss gently to mix. Spoon the fruit mixture into the pineapple shells. Garnish with the reserved whole strawberries.

 TIPS FROM OUR KITCHEN

Unlike many fruits, pineapple does not become sweeter after it has been picked. When shopping, find a pineapple with a plump shape then smell the stem end; it should smell sweet and aromatic, not heavy or fermented. Avoid pineapples with mold, bruises or dark, watery "eyes."

A thin paring knife or grapefruit knife works well for cutting the pineapple from the shell to make the serving boats.

Turn this into a main dish salad by adding smoked turkey, ham or cooked chicken to the fruit mixture.

If you want the rum flavor without the alcohol, substitute ½ teaspoon rum flavoring mixed with ½ cup pineapple juice.

Nutrition Analysis *(Per Serving)*: Calories: 132 / Cholesterol: 0 mg / Carbohydrates: 25 g / Protein: 1 g / Sodium: 2 mg / Fat: 1 g (Saturated Fat: 0 g) / Potassium: 261 mg.

FRESH PINEAPPLE AND STRAWBERRIES IN SHELLS

FRESH FRUIT TRIFLE

FRESH FRUIT TRIFLE

♦ · ♦ · ♦

Beckie Domanico and her husband are real fruit lovers, and they've been enjoying Beckie's recipe for Fresh Fruit Trifle for years. For a lower-fat version, Beckie suggests substituting low- or non-fat yogurt and sour cream. She also suggests varying the type of cookies used in the recipe.

Beckie Domanico
Seasoned with Love
McAlpin's Crestview Hills
Crestview Hills
KENTUCKY

1 In a very large bowl, gently stir together the pears, apples, strawberries, kiwi fruit, grapes and oranges.

2 In small bowl, stir together the yogurt and sour cream.

3 In a 3-quart serving bowl, place ½ *cup* of the broken cookies. Spoon *one-fourth* of the fruit mixture on top. Cover with *one fourth* of the yogurt mixture.

4 Repeat, layering the cookies, fruit and yogurt mixtures. Garnish with additional broken cookies, if desired. Serve immediately or within 1 hour.

 TIPS FROM OUR KITCHEN

To break the cookies coarsely, place them in a self-sealing plastic bag. Partially seal, leaving one section of the seal open to allow air to escape. Gently roll a rolling pin over the bag until the desired texture is achieved.

This trifle can be made up to 2 hours before serving. If you plan to do so, however, dip the apples and pears in diluted lemon juice to prevent them from turning brown.

Amaretti (or amarettini) are crisp, almond-flavored macaroons usually imported from Italy. Look for them in specialty food shops.

For easier party serving, layer the cookies, fruit and yogurt mixtures in sherbet or plastic punch glasses. Garnish each with a small cookie or a sprig of fresh mint.

To section a peeled orange: Hold the orange over a bowl to catch the juices. Cut between one fruit section and the membrane, cutting to the center of the fruit. Turn the knife and slide it up the other side of the section next to the membrane; repeat. Remove any seeds from the fruit sections.

Nutrition Analysis (*Per Serving*): Calories: 213 / Cholesterol: 8 mg / Carbohydrates: 33 g / Protein: 4 g / Sodium: 35 mg / Fat: 8 g (Saturated Fat: 2 g) / Potassium: 393 mg.

recipe index

Metric Cooking Hints

By making a few conversions, cooks in Australia, Canada, and the United Kingdom can use the recipes in *America's Best-Loved Community Cookbook Recipes: Brunches & Lunches* with confidence. The charts on this page provide a guide for converting measurements from the U.S. customary system, which is used throughout this book, to the imperial and metric systems. There also is a conversion table for oven temperatures to accommodate the differences in oven calibrations.

Volume and Weight: Americans traditionally use cup measures for liquid and solid ingredients. The chart (top right) shows the approximate imperial and metric equivalents. If you are accustomed to weighing solid ingredients, here are some helpful approximate equivalents.
■ 1 cup butter, caster sugar, or rice = 8 ounces = about 250 grams
■ 1 cup flour = 4 ounces = about 125 grams
■ 1 cup icing sugar = 5 ounces = about 150 grams
   Spoon measures are used for smaller amounts of ingredients. Although the size of the tablespoon varies slightly among countries. However, for practical purposes and for recipes in this book, a straight substitution is all that's necessary.
   Measurements made using cups or spoons should always be level, unless stated otherwise.

Product Differences: Most of the ingredients called for in the recipes in this book are available in English-speaking countries. However, some are known by different names. Here are some common American ingredients and their possible counterparts:
■ Sugar is granulated or caster sugar.
■ Powdered sugar is icing sugar.
■ All-purpose flour is plain household flour or white flour. When self-rising flour is used in place of all-purpose flour in a recipe that calls for leavening, omit the leavening agent (baking soda or baking powder) and salt.
■ Light corn syrup is golden syrup.
■ Cornstarch is cornflour.
■ Baking soda is bicarbonate of soda.
■ Vanilla is vanilla essence.

Useful Equivalents

⅛ teaspoon = 0.5ml	⅔ cup = 5 fluid ounces = 150ml
¼ teaspoon = 1ml	¾ cup = 6 fluid ounces = 175ml
½ teaspoon = 2 ml	1 cup = 8 fluid ounces = 250ml
1 teaspoon = 5 ml	2 cups = 1 pint
¼ cup = 2 fluid ounces = 50ml	2 pints = 1 litre
⅓ cup = 3 fluid ounces = 75ml	½ inch = 1 centimetre
½ cup = 4 fluid ounces = 125ml	1 inch = 2 centimetres

Baking Pan Sizes

American	Metric
8x1½-inch round baking pan	20x4-centimetre sandwich or cake tin
9x1½-inch round baking pan	23x3.5-centimetre sandwich or cake tin
11x7x1½-inch baking pan	28x18x4-centimetre baking pan
13x9x2-inch baking pan	32.5x23x5-centimetre baking pan
12x7½x2-inch baking dish	30x19x5-centimetre baking pan
15x10x2-inch baking pan	38x25.5x2.5-centimetre baking pan (Swiss roll tin)
9-inch pie plate	22x4- or 23x4-centimetre pie plate
7- or 8-inch springform pan	18- or 20-centimetre springform or loose-bottom cake tin
9x5x3-inch loaf pan	23x13x6-centimetre or 2-pound narrow loaf pan or paté tin
1½-quart casserole	1.5-litre casserole
2-quart casserole	2-litre casserole

Oven Temperature Equivalents

Farenheit Setting	Celsius Setting*	Gas Setting
300°F	150°C	Gas Mark 2
325°F	160°C	Gas Mark 3
350°F	180°C	Gas Mark 4
375°F	190°C	Gas Mark 5
400°F	200°C	Gas Mark 6
425°F	220°C	Gas Mark 7
450°F	230°C	Gas Mark 8
Broil		Grill

Electric and gas ovens may be calibrated using Celsius. However, increase the Celsius setting 10 to 20 degrees when cooking above 160°C with an electric oven. For convection or forced-air ovens (gas or electric), lower the temperature setting 10°C when cooking at all heat levels.